Elemental South

Elemental South

AN ANTHOLOGY OF
SOUTHERN NATURE WRITING

Edited by Dorinda G. Dallmeyer

The University of Georgia Press
Athens and London

*Acknowledgments for the use of previously published
material appear on page xvi, which constitutes an extension
of the copyright page.*

© 2004 by the University of Georgia Press
Athens, Georgia 30602
www.ugapress.org
All rights reserved
Designed by Sandra Strother Hudson
Set in Cycles by Bookcomp, Inc.
Printed digitally in the United States of America

Library of Congress Cataloging-in-Publication Data
Elemental South : an anthology of southern nature writing /
edited by Dorinda G. Dallmeyer.
xvi, 153 p. ; 22 cm.
ISBN-13: 978-0-8203-2689-4, ISBN-10: 0-8203-2689-5 (pbk. : alk.
paper) — ISBN-13: 978-0-8203-2665-8, ISBN-10: 0-8203-2665-8
(hardcover : alk. paper)
1. Nature—Literary collections. 2. Natural history—Southern
States—Literary collections. 3. American literature—Southern
States. 4. Southern States—Literary collections. I. Dallmeyer,
Dorinda G.
PS509.N3E43   2004
810.8'036'0975—22   2004-7411

British Library Cataloging-in-Publication Data available

Contents

Foreword

Our Mutual Friend,
June 27, 1941–December 8, 2002

All of us in this book have had good conversations—sometimes semipublic and semiformal, sometimes over a cup of coffee at the airport. For a variety of reasons, Jim Kilgo and I in particular got a lot of chances to talk, and lately, of course, those talks have been much in my mind. Sometimes it would be at his house or my house, but more often at some place where we both happened to be, presumably because we were writers who belonged to the same obscure subspecies. So we would talk about our subspecific aspirations, responsibilities, grievances, and so forth. We came to no conclusions and didn't much want to. It seemed that our disagreements—mannerly, as lucid as we could make them, candid, with a certain amount of teasing back and forth—were the whole point. In a strictly religious sense, and in broader ways as well, he was a believer and I was a skeptic. But there was a lot of common ground. We grew up in small South Carolina towns, not very far or very different from each other. He was kin to people who were kin to people who were kin to me. We were of the same generation, had the same sort of boyhoods, which we had been careful not to let lapse, went to similar sorts of colleges, and loved a lot of the same books.

One of the things Jim and I did agree on was anecdote. It was the meat and drink of conviviality, the antidote to solemnity, the place where thinking got started or where it ended up. So maybe it will be all right to relate this anecdote. Not quite three years before Jim died, our friend John Lane brought a bunch of his Wofford students down to Darlington County to spend a week in January canoeing on Black Creek, looking into its human and natural history. Jim and I got to join the flotilla for one day of the trip.

We were putting the canoes in where a county road crossed the creek—a dozen or so students, six or seven canoes, a fairly steep bank, everybody full of goodwill and advice, and this beautiful, quick, black-water stream in the spring sunshine. Jim was having a pretty good day. While all the fussing around was in progress, he sat on the bank and seemed to be relaxing in a concentrated sort of way, like a boxer between rounds. But also like a turtle on a log, just soaking up being alive, noticing nothing and thinking of nothing.

But noticing and thinking were habitual to him, and when time came for us to get into the canoes, he pulled me aside and pointed to the bridge. It was one of those little low flatland bridges that don't even make a bump in the road; on high water, you'd have to duck to pass under it.

What he pointed at was some graffiti spray-painted onto the side of the bridge. Whoever did it had lain on the bridge, reached over the side, and spray-painted the letters in that awkward upside-down fashion. There were three statements. Each appeared written by a different hand. The first said:

TATER FISH HERE. MAY 11, 1999.

The second said:

DIED. MAY 15.

The third said:

ROCK AND ROLL FOR HIM.

Jim and I wound up in the same canoe, him in the bow and me in the stern. He had grown up along Black Creek, and I believe that it, more than anyplace else, was his place of genesis. He talked about it—stories, histories, fishing holes. And every now and then he would turn around, apropos of nothing in the conversation, and look at me and say it again, almost under his breath, chuckling and shaking his head, relishing the words one more time, just one more time: *Rock and Roll for Him.*

Franklin Burroughs

Preface

In describing what it meant to be a writer in the South, Flannery O'Connor wrote:

> The things we see, hear, smell, and touch affect us long before we believe anything at all, and the South impresses its image on us from the moment we are able to distinguish one sound from another. . . . This discovery of being bound through the senses to a particular society and a particular history, to particular sounds and a particular idiom, is for the writer the beginning of a recognition that first puts his work into real human perspective.

All across the South we need better ways to help people understand that to be fully human means to be engaged with our landscapes and their native communities. One key to moving toward sustainability will be to move people to action through the written word.

In an effort to meet the challenge of protecting the natural environment of the South, a group of nature writers has met since the late 1990s to discuss how they can better use their art to conserve southern landscapes. Working with these writers, Janisse Ray and I developed a vision for a series of events that would not only allow them to convene again in 2002 but also to use that assembled talent to stimulate more and better writing about nature in the South. This multifaceted Southern Nature Project included a live radio broadcast, public readings on the University of Georgia campus, a daylong workshop for aspiring nature writers, and a radio series on nature writing for national broadcast. This anthology is another manifestation of the effort we began in 2002 and presents new prose and poetry as well as previously published works.

Unlike other regions of the United States, the South has not had a long tradition of nature writing. Indeed *The Woods Stretched for Miles*, published in 1999, is credited as the first anthology of distinctly southern nature writing. This volume seeks to build on that foundation. Like Flannery O'Connor, some of the contributing authors are native southerners; whether they continue to reside in the region or not, they remain attached to it through firsthand experience. Others are southerners by choice. All have a strong sense of place bounded by history and ecological identity, wonder and awe.

The selections are grouped around the four elements: earth, air, fire, and water. It would be a mistake to see this choice of organizational motif as a simple reflection of the antebellum fascination with Classical Greece (a main product of which may have been the proliferation of Athenses and Spartas across the region). Long before European settlers arrived, these same elements appear as clan symbology among the earliest Native Americans inhabiting the South. More broadly in the world, these four elements are repeated in Chinese and Indian philosophical texts, in Celtic myth, in creation stories of the Polynesians, the Bantus, and the Australian Aborigines. Thus, in framing this anthology around these four elements, we honor that seemingly instinctual need of *Homo sapiens* to categorize our natural world, and this particular place we call home.

Commonly in creation stories, Earth is absent in the beginning and must be brought up out of the waters to sustain a people and their animal and plant companions. Earth also appears in the form of sacred mountains, real mountains found and consecrated in the landscape. In this part of the anthology, the authors examine the earth's ability to nurture us physically and spiritually, what it means to be native to a place, and how our modern lifestyle has uprooted us from our vital connection to terrain.

Air encompasses the wind and the sky, with sound and scent borne by the breeze. In this section, the authors explore the impact of air on earth-bound humans and the equally human longing to join the creatures of the air.

Fire seems the most elusive and untamable of the elements. To conjure fire to life by twirling sassafras against poplar is prestidigitation of the highest caliber. Fire warms and brightens the dark but illuminates also through rituals of propitiation and transformation, themes underlying the selections in this part of the anthology.

Water—so vital to life and yet so mutable in form—reflects the simultaneous complexity and simplicity of the natural world. Water appears in quantities menacing and benign, in immersions terrifying and divine, capable of cloaking our sins or washing them clean. Just as water connects the mountains to the sea, it connects generations across time. This image of water as a medium of purification, of connection and community, and, ultimately, of courage and hope, concludes this part of the anthology.

However skillful and moving these selections may be as exemplars of the writer's art, this anthology's aim goes beyond capturing a region's seasons through the senses. Only rarely are authors afforded the opportunity to pair their work with a personal call to action. In the epilogue, "Why We Write," eleven of the anthology's contributors explore in newly commissioned essays why writing about southern nature is important, both to them personally and to the region as a whole. These essays offer ways to be courageous enough to envision a better world and to inspire each of us to tell our own stories about our own places.

Our own places do matter, no matter how unspectacular they may appear to be. We need no better reminder of the importance of place as we mark in 2004 the sesquicentennial of the publication of *Walden*, Thoreau's loving elevation of a nondescript pond into a metaphor for wildness and wholeness. In reflecting on our own places here in the South, we can imagine new stories that will teach us how to lead more human, more profound, and more meaningful lives that will conserve our southern environment for generations yet to come.

Dorinda G. Dallmeyer

Acknowledgments

Three primary sponsors at the University of Georgia shared the management of the Southern Nature Project. The Environmental Ethics Certificate Program was the first program of its kind in the United States. Since 1983, it has grown to include forty-eight faculty members from twenty-six departments working with seventy-five graduate and undergraduate students. WUGA-FM, our National Public Radio affiliate station, and its station manager, Davin Welter, have enthusiastically supported the live productions associated with this project. The University of Georgia Sea Grant College Program, directed by Mac Rawson, has as part of its mission a focus on the sustainable use and conservation of our coastal resources. Sea Grant program staff members George Davidson and Charlotte Ingram played an integral role in the production of the live radio broadcast. A note of special thanks goes to Sea Grant's David Bryant. His love of wild Georgia began on the banks of the Ocmulgee River and continues to this day. He's a man I'm proud to call friend.

I would like to thank the following collaborators: Judith Ortiz Cofer of the UGA Creative Writing Program, Betty Jean Craige of the UGA Center for Humanities and Arts, and the University of Georgia Press. I am particularly grateful for the help and encouragement of Christa Frangiamore and Sarah McKee. The Southern Nature Project was supported by grants from REM Athens/LLC and the Lyndhurst Foundation of Chattanooga, Tennessee.

Janisse Ray has been indispensable muse and midwife for this entire undertaking. The contributing writers have embraced this project wholeheartedly and have given so generously of their time and talent. These authors are not only people worth reading; they are people worth knowing.

The editor and publisher gratefully acknowledge the following publishers and publications in which these selections first appeared:

"Black Drink" by James Kilgo is transcribed from a live reading at the University of Georgia Chapel on April 24, 2002, and is an excerpt from the more extensive treatment of the theme found in "Place of the Black Drink Tree," in *Ossabaw* (University of Georgia Press, 2004).

Ann Fisher-Wirth's poems appear in *Blue Window* (Archer Books, 2003). "Sweetgum Country" also appeared in *Valparaiso Poetry Review*. "Where, beneath the Magnolia" was published by *Gloria Mundi*.

"Eating," from *The Hermit's Story* by Rick Bass. Copyright © 2002 by Rick Bass. Reprinted by permission of Houghton Mifflin Company and Methuen Publishing Limited. All rights reserved.

All three poems by John Lane appeared originally in *The Lawson's Fork: Headwaters to Confluence* (Spartanburg, S.C.: Hub City Writers Project, 2000).

"You Are What You Eat" and "Sun Time" by Thomas Rain Crowe were published previously in the *Smoky Mountain News*.

"Islands," "Air," "Fire in the Path," and "Water" by Christopher Camuto were excerpted from *Another Country* (University of Georgia Press, 2000).

"Into the Dragon's Mouth," from *Wind: How the Flow of Air Has Shaped Life, Myth, and the Land* by Jan DeBlieu. Copyright © 1998 by Jan DeBlieu. Reprinted by permission of Houghton Mifflin Company. All rights reserved.

"Built by Fire," in *Ecology of a Cracker Childhood* (Minneapolis: Milkweed Editions, 1999). Copyright © 1999 by Janisse Ray. Reprinted with permission from Milkweed Editions.

"Home," "Rock Springs," and "The White Heron" are reprinted from *Living on Wilderness Time* by Melissa Walker (Charlottesville, Va.: University of Virginia Press, 2002) with the kind permission of the University of Virginia Press.

"Diving into the Heart of a Poem" was adapted from Bill Belleville's book *River of Lakes: A Journey on Florida's St. Johns River* (University of Georgia Press, 2000). "Bears" was adapted from an essay first published in *Oxford American*.

Earth

day I would find a small village of Creek Indians who had been living in secret. I combed the woods for signs of the people who once lived there; though I occasionally found arrowheads, I never found bones or pottery shards, let alone the live Indians of my mind's eye. With long braids, sun-bronzed skin, and a headdress my mother made from hawk feathers I found in the fields, I thought of myself as an Indian girl.

From an early age I lived in two worlds: the rough-and-tumble world of the outdoors and the ladylike world of dress up and tea parties. Although I wore patent-leather shoes, organdy dresses, and white gloves to Sunday school and fancy birthday parties, I have practically no memories of those events. I do remember catching and cooking crawfish and bringing home a leathery egg I'd found in the bushes by the house.

"Snake egg," my mother said, and together we sliced into the egg and poured out a blue snake shape swimming in what looked like the white of a chicken egg. With my mother's blessing, I buried the remains in the pet cemetery in the backyard. For my mother all life was sacred. For my father a snake was a snake, as my growing collection of rattles proved. Once I stuck my head inside the hollow of a large tree and saw what appeared to be dozens of rattlesnakes all coiled up together in a large pile. There may have been only a few, four or five or so, but the sight of those snakes is one of my strongest and scariest memories.

It was my mother who taught me to pay attention to birds. I must have been a toddler when she first pointed out the common backyard birds: blue jays, cardinals, brown thrashers, and mockingbirds. Then came bluebirds, woodpeckers, vultures, and hawks. Walking across the field toward the woods, I would look to the sky for a red-tailed hawk or a turkey buzzard. Soon I learned to recognize the little birds—titmice, nuthatches, and chickadees. The arrival of cedar waxwings or a flock of goldfinches was a celebratory event that Mother announced to the family and neighbors. She had a knack for finding birds on nests, and when she did she would tell me where they were, swearing me to secrecy. On summer evenings we would watch robins and house wrens tending their broods. When a neighborhood cat nailed a fledgling, I felt the terror of predation as only a small child can.

Birds for my father were another matter. Quails, doves, ducks, wild turkeys, and geese were prized prey, and when on a crisp fall day my father came home with the pockets of his hunting jacket full of dove or quail, I joined in the ritual of plucking feathers and removing the entrails of what would be the best part of a celebratory meal. While I hated what seemed to be the cat's senseless wasting of a newly fledged wren, I wasn't troubled that my father killed, my mother cooked, and we all ate birds. Yet I learned to whistle at an early age, and I loved to mimic the bobwhite's call and to listen for a response.

I wouldn't say I was a tomboy, though I walked the thin line between doing what is required of a southern lady and following the dictates of nature. My maternal grandmother taught me how. She loved the woods and swamps of rural Georgia. At Thanksgiving she would gather family and friends for an elaborate campout at the mouth of Turkey Creek, and each June everybody would go to the Ogeechee River Swamp for serious fishing. Whenever the fishing was really good, however, she would take off alone or with a friend, pushing off in a rowboat into Flanders Lake, Rocky Creek, or one of several small ponds in the area. Often on a weekday, with no one else around, she would spend hours fishing, and usually she caught a nice string of trout, bream, or redbreast, which she would then bring home for supper. Once when I was with her, our boat was suddenly surrounded by several large, hideous water moccasins attempting to feed on the string of fish we were trailing. When I cried out to my grandmother that the snakes were after us, she snapped at me, insisting that they wouldn't hurt me.

My grandmother was a true southern lady. She had graduated from college, read George Eliot, played a mean game of bridge, raised roses, secured her silk dresses at the throat with a diamond bar pin, and coiled her long braids queenlike on the top of her head. But she was happiest camping out at the mouth of Turkey Creek or paddling out to the other side of an isolated pond early in the morning, or whenever the fish were biting. Never mind that she couldn't swim. She taught me that to do what you want to do requires taking risks. I can still imagine her voice when I get in a tight spot.

"Those snakes aren't interested in you, and we're not going to turn this boat over. So calm down and start paddling."

To most southerners, home is the place where they were born and grew up. Like many people my age in the South, I lived in one place until I left to go to college, and that place is the center of a larger geographical area extending from the Georgia Sea Islands and the Okefenokee Swamp in the south to the Appalachian Mountains in the north. Even though I have lived in the same house in Atlanta with Jerome and our children for more than a quarter of a century, our house there is only one of many linked elements that all together comprise home.

Home is the sun setting behind a cotton field, a cold-water spring bubbling out of the ground and flowing into a river swamp, a small pond surrounded with cypress, and a red-clay road winding through acres and acres of pines. Home is a stand of blooming peach trees in the spring and a pecan orchard raining nuts all over the ground in the fall. It's a towering oak tree I planted as a seedling and the antique rose that's the last remnant of my grandmother's once carefully tended garden. Home is the way the trees grow, the land lies, and the scent of a skunk or honeysuckle lingers in still air. Home is the past, memory, a time gone by. Home is more than the sum of its parts, more than a house, a river, cotton fields, red clay, a wild rose, or fat little pecans hiding in wet leaves.

Before I went away for the first time, I would have said that Jerome and I have stayed in the South out of a sense of obligation to be near our parents. Now it seems we stayed in Georgia because we felt pulled to be there; we *wanted* to be there. When people I met asked where my home was, I simply said, "Georgia," and I said it with feeling. It would be a long time before I'd learn that it's possible to hold that intense attachment to one place in tension with a passion for other places and other ways of life.

JAMES KILGO

Black Drink

When I awoke, I went out for a walk, taking a lane that started at the back of the Main House compound and ran south through longleaf and live oak woods. It was cool enough for a jacket, but I had left mine in my room and didn't want to go back for it. A deer stepped from the woods into the aisle up ahead, realized its mistake, and darted into the brush on the other side, but a litter of busy piglets—some red, some banded, most black—allowed me to walk right up on them before they scattered squealing through the rattling palmettos. After a mile or so, the lane brought me to a tidal creek running shallow between steep banks. A bridge had once spanned the channel, but it was long since swept away, and only skeletal pilings, encrusted with coon oysters, were left standing in the water. Unwilling to get my feet wet, I sat down on the bank and took out an apple. There was a late afternoon stillness in the woods. The birds were silent, and the tide was almost out.

Across the creek lay the rest of Ossabaw—ocean beach, salt marsh, palmetto jungle, and maritime forest, stretching seven or eight miles southward—the raw material of the story I had thought I would write. All it would take was an act of imagination and God only knew how many days of walking. Something flapped within my chest, like a bird in a cage when it's time to fly south.

I had discovered while still a child that in order to appropriate any part of the natural world, I had to do something with it—learn the names of birds and flowers, make drawings of them, carve them in wood, and, when the birds and animals were legal game, hunt them. A friend once asked me why I couldn't be content simply to sit in the woods and enjoy God's creation without having to take something home. The answer to that is the verb *appropriate*, which means to take possession of. As arrogant as it may seem to pick and press a wildflower or to hunt and kill a deer, even for the table, what I wanted was not so much the flower or the

8

venison as an experience that would transform the place where it happened into a story. Such experience of, or relationship with, a specific place seems to me the circumstance in which we evolved. To be deprived of it, as most Americans are, may be to live outside our natural habitat and consequently to suffer the anxiety of exile.

A yaupon holly stood on the opposite bank—a large tree for that species and still covered with red berries. Maybe I could collect the leaves and brew me a batch of black drink. I was in the right place for it. *Ossabaw* is a Muskogean-Hitchiti word said to have meant "place of the black drink tree" or "where yaupon holly grows"—not a particularly romantic name until you learn what black drink was: a strongly caffeinated, dark brown tea brewed from the dried leaves and twigs of the holly, *Ilex vomitoria*, and used by Indians throughout the Mississippian culture to purify body, mind, and spirit. So strong was its medicine that only men drank it. They made a ritual of it, consuming it in preparation for council meetings or war or to entertain important guests. They drank it hot, from decorated conch shells, in great quantities, until they began to sweat profusely and finally to vomit. The tree grows naturally throughout the southeastern coastal plain, but this island, as far as we know, was the only place that bore its name. Whatever virtue the drink possessed, whatever essence of Ossabaw, remained available, inherent in the leaves of the tree across the creek. A draught of black drink, drunk hot from a left-handed conch, might be good medicine for what ailed me, or, better, a quick way for me to ingest the wild spirit of the island.

I all but laughed at myself. That notion was too romantic even for me. From the right, foraging down the creek in my direction, came three black pigs—young animals, hardly more than shoats—and their cloven hooves were leaving cookie-cutter tracks in the firm sand. On they came, snuffling quietly among themselves, earnest in their search for something to eat. Their long snouts were gray with dried mud and their sparse coats were matted with it. A light breeze was in my favor, but the slightest movement of my hand would send them grunting for cover. Directly beneath me now, they stopped, suddenly confused, and looked at each other. Their soft grunts sounded inquisitive: Did anyone smell a man? One of them must have said yes, for they bolted, scampering up the side of the opposite bank and into the palmettos.

I got to my feet, my dreams of wild Ossabaw smudged by the appearance of piney-wood rooters. The island was overrun by feral swine; one saw them everywhere, for the most part small and black like these but some were red and some belted, betraying barnyard blood. Where they had come from was a matter of controversy, an academic argument with serious practical consequences. I. Lehr Brisbin, a populations geneticist who has studied Ossabaw pigs, had told me that swine first came onto Ossabaw in the seventeenth and eighteenth centuries, brought from Europe as a food supply by Spanish explorers and missionaries. That original breed was a small, slab-sided, long-snouted, bluish gray animal called Mangalitza. Brisbin believed that a remnant population survived on the sea islands until the islands were bought and planted in cotton and rice by antebellum planters, who introduced porcine stock of their own to help feed their slaves. Pigs survived the demise of plantation culture as they had survived the departure of the Spanish, and by the twentieth century they had established themselves as part of the island fauna. As a result of their long and isolated feral history, Brisbin said, Ossabaw pigs had developed unique biochemistry. They had learned, for example, to tolerate a high degree of salt in their food and drinking water. Because long-term feral populations of *Sus scrofa* rarely occur anywhere, he thought it essential that at least some of the Ossabaw pigs be protected. The Department of Natural Resources, on the other hand, was not buying Brisbin's argument. They pointed to red and belted pigs as evidence of recent introductions of recognizable domestic breeds— ordinary feral swine, trash animals, like starlings. But wherever they had come from, said the DNR, they were not native to Ossabaw, and they were doing irreparable damage to the environment, uprooting important plants and raiding turtle nests.

Not being a biologist, I had no basis for judging who was right, but one thing was clear: as wild as the pigs had grown, they remained relics of human activity, or to be accurate, of the Euro-American presence on Ossabaw. With pigs running all over the place, it was impossible to maintain the illusion that Ossabaw was pristine wilderness. The Torreys and Sandy West had allowed the island to revert to a natural condition, but it would never be home again to wolves and panthers. A complete book on Ossabaw would have to take that into account, not just the absence of great predators and virgin maritime forest but also the causes of such depredations—in other words, the four-hundred-year-old record of negotiations between people and nature, the effects of this environment on repeated attempts at settlement and the effects of settlement on the island. Indeed, Ossabaw might be read as a microcosm of the European presence in the Garden of North America, and pigs struck me as the perfect symbol of that presence, an ugly knot that tied together the cultural and the natural history, and provided me with access to both, a way into the narrative. Moreover, as a foreign invader with explosive reproductive capacity, the swine population reminded me of blight if not of cancer, and the island a host organism that so far had found ways of surviving. I wondered if the poet Gerard Manley Hopkins was right when he said, "And for all this, nature is never spent: / There lives the dearest freshness deep down things."

One way to find out might be to take off my boots and wade across the creek and follow those pigs wherever they took me. But, Lord, I thought, it's a big island. And I was tired, whether from my illness or the hormone treatment or the residue of fifty-eight years, I didn't know. With little resistance I entertained the dangerous question, why write anyway? Though you may have stumbled on a way to experience the island as a story in which you can participate if you have time enough and energy, to what purpose is the effort at this late hour?

Just then something stirred in the leaves across the creek. The late afternoon sun was shafting through the canopy, spotlighting palmetto fans, and amidst that light and shadow, partly concealed by foliage, stood a pig of a silver color. My eyes widened. Who had ever heard of such a thing? It was of moderate size—a grown animal—and it almost gleamed. I stepped forward for a better look, but just as an image reflected on water is broken into a thousand flakes by a sudden gust, so the silver pig disintegrated in a shift of light and shadow that rustled the undergrowth.

In the notes I wrote that night, I first described the pig as "numinous," a word I use to mean something like "possessing an unearthly or supernatural glow." But I wanted to be scientific and objective, and this after all was a pig I was talking about. So I struck through the word. Obviously, the illusion of silver was nothing more than a trick of sunlight. On the other hand, the trick required a pig of unusual color, a steel-dust blue, which is rare among swine—so rare, in fact, that I have seen it used only to describe the ancient Mangalitzas—and that was reason enough, I decided, to write the word in again. But I thought I'd better look it up before I did. The first definition in *The American Heritage Dictionary* was not much help: "Of or pertaining to a numen." Unfamiliar with that form of the word, I checked it out: "A presiding divinity or spirit of a place." That sent me to the etymology in *The Oxford English Dictionary*. *Numen*, I found, comes from the Latin *numen*, which means "a divinity," but *numen* itself was somehow associated in the ancient Roman mind with *nuere*, which means simply "a nod." There was nothing in any of this to support my personal definition of "an unearthly or supernatural glow," a notion that must have come from the influence on my unconscious mind of *luminous*. So I was stuck with an obscure association between "divinity" and "nod," until a friend who loves words suggested to me that a divinity may be understood as one who nods in approval. Yes. In that case, an original pig plated silver by the sun is about as numinous as a pig can hope to be.

ANN FISHER-WIRTH

Where, beneath the Magnolia

for Teresa Washington

Wind shakes
the shabby cedars,
gusts and torments blowing up
harder and harder
over the mosses of Rowan Oak—
where the brick-laid maze,
derelict now, beautiful,
circled the ancient magnolia,
eaten and hollowed
and finally last year storm-stricken,
now only a pile of black shards and leafmeal—
where once Teresa stood
in sweat-shimmering August,
in a bower of whispering
branches,
and spoke with Caroline Barr
in tongues and rattles and honeyed
groanings. Fern-furred
branches bowed
above the burnished
river their voices
conjured, Teresa deep
in her Ifá trance
speaking with Caroline,
dead since 1940—with the woman
behind the book,
the woman
behind the word,

whom Teresa, unafraid,
could spell from the monstrous
shadows. Tongues
and echoes, blue buzzings
in the honeysuckle,
snail-shine and humus
beneath them . . . bracken,
bloodroot, mutterings
in the air—they spoke
and were not
as they'd been spoken.
How can I say
what passed between them
in the rising wind?
What blossoms
has no name.

Rowan Oak is William Faulkner's house in Oxford, Mississippi; Caroline Barr was the
woman he called Mammy, to whom he dedicated *Go Down Moses*.

Eating

Sometime before dawn, on their first date, driving north through North Carolina to go canoeing in the mountains, they hit an owl. Sissy was sitting up, leaning against Russell's shoulder, and they had been listening to the radio, not speaking, benumbed by the lateness of the hour and the endless roll of road beneath.

They saw the underside of the owl flare up, brilliant white in the glare of the headlights—it swooped right at their faces, barely missing the windshield—and then there was half an instant of silence, so that they thought they had missed it (it was a great horned owl and seemed as large and incongruous to the night sky in that brief moment as a flying man), but then they heard and felt the thump of the large body striking the canoe, and a few feathers swirled past their windshield, and after slowing and looking back, not seeing it, they drove on, remorseful, saddened.

"Maybe he made it," Russell said.

They followed narrow winding mountain roads that hugged steep cliffs and the edges of rivers, from which rose ribbons of steam. They drove slower and slower and saw more and more owls, passing through them as if through a nighttime hatch of immense moths, though they didn't strike any more.

They were still in North Carolina when the sun came up, burning orange-red through the fog, and they stopped for breakfast at a small diner that had a smokehouse attached to its side, through the wood-slat cracks of which issued slow blue smoke. The scent of the smoke caught their attention as if a clothesline had been strung across the road.

The diner was built from old cinder blocks and the parking lot was red clay with scattered beds of gravel. Numerous low swales held muddy water. The lot was filled with old mud-splattered trucks and cars, bald-tired and with sprung-out taillights and headlights duct-taped in place. All of the license plates were local, and none of the vehicles had bumper stickers of any kind—as if the drivers led lives so pure as to be unconcerned about anything beyond their immediate control.

Russell and Sissy went out back first to take a look at what was cooking. They found glistening pork ribs and ham steaks blushing as red as oak leaves in autumn. Some chickens, too.

"I'm hungry," Russell said. They stood there in the blue smoke, letting it bathe them for a while, and looked out at the forest dropping away below them: sweetgum, hickory, oak, loblolly, mountain laurel. They could see more ridges, more knolls and valleys, gold lit, through the framework of green leaves and branches. Tobacco country, down in the lowlands. Russell took another look at the hams. "This is my country," he said. "Or getting real near it."

He turned and studied the mound of fresh-split oak sitting next to the grill. Fuel for the coming day's work of altering the taste of a thing. He didn't possess a trace of fat. It would be hard to guess where the calories went on him. It was his own opinion that they just sort of vaporized, like coal or some other combustible shoved into a glowing furnace.

When they went inside, the diners all swiveled to study them unabashedly, and at length. Sissy had never felt so on display. Old farmers in blue denim overalls and straw hats staring at her through Coke-bottle glasses. Canes. Gap-teeth, gold teeth, tobacco teeth. Finally Sissy felt compelled to speak. "Hello," she said.

One of the old farmers gestured the nub of a finger toward Russell, and then toward their car, and toward the canoe perched atop it.

"Son," he said, "what are you doin' with that owl?"

They looked out the window and saw that an owl, bent-looking and ruffled, was sitting on the hood of their car, blinking. It had gotten sucked up into the canoe, and Russell had been driving so fast it must have ridden pinned back in the stern, unable to get out. Now that the car had stopped and the pressure had been released, the owl seemed scarcely able to believe it was free.

"Can it fly?" one of the old men asked. Others were staring at Russell now.

"We must have scooped it out of the sky," Russell said.

Only about half of them believed him. They set their papers down and sipped their coffee and watched the owl with interest and speculation. "It seems disinclined to fly," one of the men said.

"Hit's watching us back," said another, and now it seemed as if a gauntlet had been laid down, so that there was no way the old men would let the owl—this ruffled, yellow-eyed interloper—outstare them, and they crouched forward, leaning over their steaming cups of coffee, and surveyed the owl, which was still squatting in similar fashion, hunch-shouldered, as suspicious of the events that had brought him to this place as were the old men.

Sissy and Russell settled in to eat: road-weary and ravenous, they settled slowly, firmly, back into the real world. Russell could not decide what to exclude from the menu, so he ordered one of everything—pancakes, grits, ham, fried eggs, ribs, bacon, biscuits, gravy—and as if to counterbalance his gluttony, Sissy ordered a cup of coffee and a thin piece of ham.

They ate in silence. A slash of morning sunlight fell across their table, and, after so much darkness on their drive through the night, the sunlight seemed now to carry extra sweetness and clarity.

Russell finished his first helpings and decided to focus thereafter on the fried eggs and ham. The waitress brought him another plate and he stretched—the cracking of tight ligaments in his back sounded almost musical—and told the waitress she'd better just start frying eggs, and that he'd tell her when to stop.

One of the old men noticed the new plate of food and marked a little tally of it on his napkin.

Russell ate steadily for over half an hour: two eggs, ham, two eggs, ham. The restaurant ran out of eggs after he had eaten twenty-four, though they still had some ribs and ham left; but finally Russell said he had had enough, and he leaned back and stretched and patted, then thumped, the taut skin of his belly.

He reached out and took Sissy's hand fondly, and they sat there for a while alongside the old men, in the mild sunlight, and watched the owl.

"Hit wants in to eat some ham, too," one of them speculated.

"If a cat walks by, that owl'll kill it," another warned, and now they began to look about almost eagerly, hoping for such a drama.

As if bored by *not* eating, Russell decided to order a single pancake for dessert, and when it arrived he doused it with syrup and then ate it slowly, with much satisfaction, and said, "Damn, I wish I had an egg to go on top of this," and the old men laughed.

Russell finished and then got up to go to the bathroom. The waitress got on the phone and began ordering reinforcements for the larder. Sissy noticed that the phone was an old black rotary dial and felt again that they had driven into the past. The old men asked Sissy where they were from, and when Sissy said "Mississippi" the old men looked slightly troubled, as if concerned that there might be more coming just like them: invaders, insatiable infidels—a population of marauders who might devour the entire town.

In the bathroom, Russell settled in on the toilet and stared out the open window at the garden beyond. The lace curtains fluttered in the morning breeze. As Russell was gazing, a mule's enormous head appeared from out of nowhere, startling him considerably. The mule looked as if he had come to inspect something, and, not knowing what the mule wanted, Russell handed him one end of the roll of toilet paper, which the mule took in his enormous teeth and then walked away carefully, gently, drawing the toilet paper out in a steady unspooling.

Russell watched, mesmerized, as the mule wandered randomly around the garden and through the field and then around the corner, around toward the front of the restaurant, as if laying down the borders of some newly claimed territory—and it was not until the spool of paper was nearly unwound that Russell had the presence of mind to snap it off and save some for himself.

When he emerged, the old men and the waitress were staring at him as if wondering what he might do next, and he and Sissy went out and began gathering the toilet paper, even as the mule now moved along behind them, grazing on the paper.

At first the owl would not let them near their car, hissing and snapping at them, but Russell got a branch and was able to dislodge it; they watched as it launched itself hale and hearty into silent flight and disappeared, a hunter, into the woods. They waved good-bye to the old men and the waitress and drove off, and as they were leaving the parking lot they saw another truck turning in, a beat-up old red truck carrying in the back a single immense hog, which looked none too excited about the journey, as if knowing—maybe from the odor of the smokehouse—what stage of life's journey he was now entering.

"Are you always like this?" Sissy asked as they drove on farther, deeper into the mountains, anticipating the day.

"Like what?" Russell asked.

JOHN LANE

Hounds Chasing Deer in the Suburbs

Through the escaped privet along Lawson's Fork
they follow their buried intentions to the edge
of yards where the scent is lost among fescue.

There they turn, memory of houses and doors
driving them back across the street into wiry thicket,
meandering stream, muddy runnel, cut bank.

We stand and listen, leashes at the ready if only
they will circle back up the nature trail and catch
sight of their other masters and come to their senses.

But we hear their distant shadow yelps through winter
woods, which has drawn game out of the country.
They are not circling, but zigzagging after spooked deer.

Our only hope of not going home without them
is to wish the deer long gone so we can wait
out this spell of wildness crazy in their old blood.

You Are What You Eat

If it's true that you are what you eat, then this week I'm blue-berries, blackberries, cucumbers, and new potatoes. It's been a bumper year for all four and my tongue is purple, my throat is cool, and my belly is full.

Here at the tailgate market, a young girl has shown up with a large beer cooler from which she is selling recycled cartons full of the fattest blackberries you've ever seen. And Karen and Johnny White are selling them by the gallon. The blackberries will be the first thing to sell out, and soon the young girl will be over in the music tent playing fiddle tunes with Cathy Arps to a growing and enthusiastic crowd of listeners.

As I eat a handful of blackberries I got in trade from Karen and Johnny for some of the largest new potatoes I've ever grown, I'm reminded, again, of the old medicinal adage You are what you eat. I've always wondered about the origin of this phrase and just how we are supposed to take it. Are we, literally, what we eat? Common sense would lead one to believe that a healthy diet would produce a healthy person. But then, there are so many exceptions: there are those who can (and do) eat anything and are still slim, trim, and vital, as well as those who eat well and are sick. But in the end, for most of us at least, I think that what we eat plays a significant role in our overall mental and physical health. How could it not?

Here at the tailgate market we are mostly organic fruit and veg-etable growers. We grow organically not because we can charge more for our produce (in fact, most of us are charging *less* than what you'd pay for radiated and chemically induced produce at the supermarket), but because we like the rich, sweet, even loamy taste of organically grown foods, and we like knowing what goes in and on the food we put in our bodies, having some modicum of control over our lives.

Those who buy our produce would seem to agree, including the many vegetarians we see each Saturday morning here on the backstreet in Sylva, those folks who have abandoned the American obsession with eating meat for every meal and have taken to a lighter fare and are leaner for having done so—or so it would seem from outward physical appearance. There are no hogs being butchered or slabs of steak being sold here at the Sylva market—no "mad cows."

The blackberry girl and I are having fun imagining that today we *are* blackberries. We stick out our purple tongues at each other as proof of our identity and tell blackberry jokes we have made up on the spot. Of course there are the obvious allusions to chiggers, briars, and raccoon scat in our silly jokes, and we have fun passing the morning away with our happy childish banter.

A couple of truck positions down from mine, a large crowd has gathered around the honey vendors from over in Almond. And much bee talk is going on. "Talk about organic!" I hear a loud male voice proclaim. And it's true, the bees give us one of the most wonderfully and miraculously natural products known to man. Ambrosia, food of the Gods, the land of milk and honey are just some of the honey-related sayings that have been handed down to us over the ages. And, if it's true that man cannot live by bread alone, then could he, maybe, live by honey alone? With these thoughts wreaking havoc in my head, I wander over to the honey tent, make my way to the display table, and put a big plastic spoon of the early clover and wildflower honey in my mouth. Mmm. . . . The blackberry girl is there in the honey tent, too. She has beaten me there and you can see some of her "free taste" oozing out of the side of her mouth and running down her chin. We smile at each other, knowingly. Now we are honey!

JOHN LANE

The Bottomland

No one grows corn in the bottomland.
Lawson's Fork meanders between its steep banks
past saplings, over fallen saw timber

undercut sharply by slow pewter current.
We walk the trail, following the dogs,
who follow the boys on their bikes.

It is muddy, and the bottomland
is soaked through from recent winter rains.
Mud catches in the hexes on my boots.

I carry the bottomland home
and think of it on the high ridge of this city
as I scrape my dirty shoes.

Bears

There are bears in the woods around the St. Johns River today. I know because I see their tracks in the soft white sugar sand, the sign of an ancient animal on an ancient dune, miles from the sea. It is *Ursus americanus floridanus*, a subspecies of the black bear, and it is unique to Florida. I look closely and see the pads of the feet are big and full. Except for the claw marks, which cut into the sand, the tracks might almost be cartoonish, as if left by a giant, precious toy bear come to life.

But if black bears are precious—in fact, they're threatened with extinction in Florida—they're not toys. They are big, wild animals that need a lot of landscape to roam. When their territory is fragmented, the animals still lumber across these man-made boundaries just as they've been doing long before we started building roads and golden arches. At one time, the pre-Columbian Timucua—and later, Seminoles—hunted this bear on the peninsula. So did the white settlers who followed. Now, the largest single cause of mortality is road kill.

This evening, we are hunting bears, too. Except not with guns. A trap is being set to snare one of the animals. The man setting the trap is state wildlife biologist Walt McCown. Before his tenure with bears, McCown trapped and collared panthers in south Florida. But the bear seems to suit him better—perhaps it's because he's unhurried, deliberate, a bit hulking and bearlike himself.

Affixing a collar with a radio transmitter to a wild animal seems somewhat of a humiliation, the thievery of a vital part of their wildness. But it's a trade-off, allowing biologists to press for fewer roads, and where there are no such options, to argue for wildlife underpasses. Bears range for the same reasons we do—for food, comfort, and when the need arises, a warm body. They especially range at the swampy edges of the St. Johns and along the sandy limestone scarps that define the low valley of the river itself. Forested rivers like the St. Johns are natural corridors for bears, who wade its swamps and swim its waters to get where they want to be. They are safe here.

To get to this place, I have hiked down a winding trail, around wild rosemary bushes and clumps of gray deer moss, and over pine logs. "See the way you stepped over that log," drawls McCown. "A bear does the same thing. He walks flat-footed like us, doesn't want to stumble or step on anything sharp."

Today, McCown uses his knowledge of bear walking to build a foliage aisle leading up to a cable snare. Inside the aisle, he places branches and sharp sticks and, right before the snare, rolls the heel of his palm into the sand. The bear will step around the sticks, into the palm tracks, and then finally, trip the snare.

What will draw him here will be bait, which McCown is now scattering on the trail. The bait is Krispy Kreme doughnuts. "Well, if you're eating dry nuts and berries all day long," says McCown, "a Krispy Kreme is going to look pretty damn good to you."

Last season, McCown's team set more than three hundred such traps, collaring forty-seven bears. Oddly, I wonder how the paltry Wildlife Commission budgets for all those doughnuts. "We get them out of the Dumpster," says McCown. "One night, we just about came to blows with some local hog farmers who'd been using that same Dumpster for years." McCown looks up from his snare, shakes his head, looking particularly bearesque at the moment. "I could die tomorrow and say I've done it all. Come to near fisticuffs with hog farmers over Dumpster doughnuts used to trap bears."

Hibernation is coming soon, and while it's not the barren winter coma of northern bears, it is a time when the critters simply slow down, sleeping more and eating less. For certain mature females, winter is also a time to whelp two or three cubs, hidden back in some secret place, maybe in a hollow under a fallen sweetgum.

The woods on the trail around me in this season are luxuriant and alive—the oaks have dropped chubby acorns, cinnamon ferns have sent up new fiddleheads, and berries are thick on the saw palmettos. Tasty insects, like walking sticks and grasshoppers, are fat, too. It's the most active time of the year for the black bear: a season to roam in search of a mate as well as to gorge before kicking back. As if to celebrate the advent of this bruin bacchanal, wildflowers are raging in the understory—the bright purple rods of blazing star, the carnival frill of the passionflower, the cerulean blue of the celestial lily. Last night it rained, and the tracks I have seen are so new they must have been made just a few hours—or perhaps minutes—ago. Scat, which appears in great blue-black piles of berries and nuts on the trail, seems just as fresh. I look closely at the trunks of young longleaf pines for other signs, and soon, I see them too: bark has been stripped off several pine trees, as if a bear stood on its hind legs and reached up as far as it could, just like a human. On one bare trunk, the incisions of claw marks have been left behind, the signature of a male marking his turf.

I have been searching for bears for twenty years now along the St. Johns. Like all searches, it has taken me to places I never intended to go, introducing me to an authentic wilderness where, previously, I thought there was none. After all, Florida is an odd, discordant state where most tourists are lured into believing that no reality exists except in contrived theme parks or on replenished faux beaches, seen from a patio with pink umbrella drinks.

Where there is no such development, wet forest and marshlands may stretch out for miles. For newcomers used to the dramatic geology back on the continent, this lowland biological treasure seems a puzzle. It was for me, for a long time.

The trap has been set and hidden. It blends in so well with the floor of the forest that I might step into it if I hadn't seen it being created myself.

Along with two other biologists, we retreat to a dirt road a mile away and wait for darkness, the time when bears begin to move about. A light November rain begins to fall. We duck back under the canopy of a sweetgum. We are quiet, just listening to the rainfall hit the leaves.

McCown holds up a small VHF antenna, which will pick up a signal when the snare is sprung. He hears pings. "The doorbell's ringing."

We hop in a pickup and drive quickly to the snare site. Although calm by nature, the black bear doesn't much like to have his foot caught in a snare. In his madness, he will tear up everything he can reach—may even injure himself. McCown loads his tranquilizer gun and rushes down the path. It is full dark now, and raining hard.

A young male bear is in the trap. He charges as soon as he sees us. McCown pops him once, and then again. Finally, the bear topples. Although down, the animal continues to raise his head and lick the air. The biologists move in anyway. They take tissue samples, measure, and then finally weigh him using a large meat scale tied to a sand pine. He weighs 261 pounds.

This bear has an ear tag with a number on it, R021. McCown checks the tag number against a list, finds the bear lost his original collar after being hit crossing a road last year. One of the biologists feels the bear's left front leg and finds it was broken in the collision. Although healed, it's now stiff and doesn't bend as it should.

Bears share a common ancestor with dogs, and R021 looks not unlike a giant black Lab, round stout body and long, broad snout and no whiskers.

He is exhaling in great snorts, and he smells musky, feral. I lightly stroke his fur, and lifting a heavy paw, run my fingers over its pad. I likely will never get this close to a live bear again.

The drug is wearing off. We back away, and McCown throws a pail of water on the bear to sober him up. The animal staggers and then lumbers off between the palmettos in slow motion. The bear hunt is over.

As I drive away through the forest, it occurs to me that if we can figure out how to keep wide-ranging bears in the landscape, we also get a multitude of other rewards from the bargain.

If we're successful, the great ecological safety net that supports the Florida black bear might still endure, a throwback to a time when wilderness laid itself, end to end, over this entire peninsula.

There are tricks to be learned here.

Of them all, the most essential is the trick of the quiet, the art of slowing down long enough to see how bears step over logs in the forest. And to want to understand why.

ANN FISHER-WIRTH

Raccoons, a History

We watched him last summer by flashlight,
moonlight, sharp paws flickering,
thick-furred body anxious and upright—
Quick, quick, he'd dive at the cat food,
then feint and check for danger. Now it's January,
raining, death swells in the wall—
he must have come home to die last fall,
slunk off into the crawl space.
First we noticed the sweetness,
the something-not-quite-clean-here.
Was it a squirrel, a mouse? we wondered.
Weeks passed, and it didn't diminish—
Could we take the boards off? No, too old,
they would splinter. And we didn't know
for certain where the dead thing was.
So my husband climbed onto the roof
to shovel ten pounds of quicklime into the crawl space—
and found the other raccoon, the little female.
Shivering and scrawny,
she tried to squeeze into the hole
but he blocked it with his body.
He said, "She looked sad. She turned away."

Last spring they were born in the walls,
where my daughter slept in the guest room bed.
We heard them scrabbling, squeaking.
"It's beasts," I said, "are they dying?"
But she laughed like she laughed when she was little—
"Mom, listen to them, they're snuggling, they're happy."

They grew and climbed out from the roof,
played with their mother and dug through the compost,
pawed at the screen on the kitchen window.
We loved them. Then the big one
started to fight the female, scratching and snarling.
Plenty of food for both of them,
but he'd snap and slash till she cowered on the deck
with her one filched piece of cat food.

Sometime in the fall, the mother vanished.
For the big one and the female, was it sickness? Poison?

—January, raining, first came the stench,
then quicklime dusting down from between the beaded boards,
then snow, and the smell diminished.
Now lime-floured flies
drawn forth by the warmth of the kitchen
dot the walls, caress the light globes, circle and hover like ghosts,
stunned.
I vacuum them up, they're easy targets,
but wave after wave they emerge from the doorjamb.

Islands

The earth is a great island floating in a sea of water, and sus-
pended at each of the four cardinal points by a cord hanging
down from the sky vault, which is of solid rock. When the
world grows old and worn out, the people will die and the
cords will break and let the earth sink down into the ocean, and
all will be water again. The Indians are afraid of this.

JAMES MOONEY, "Myths of the Cherokee"

The Cherokee mind tends to spatialize time. This is not sur-
prising in people who do not keep a written history, a practice that
makes the cyclical appear to be linear. Among other things, this habit
of mind keeps the past at hand in only its most useful forms, which is
perhaps at the heart of what is called good medicine.

I'm facing *Duni'skwalgun'i*, an ancient word rooted in rock.

Trivial names have no power, and this is clearly a powerful place.
Mooney notes: "*Duni'skwalgun'i*—the double peak known as the Chim-
ney Tops, in the Great Smoky Mountains about the head of Deep Creek,
in Swain County, North Carolina. On the north side is the pass known as
Indian Gap. The name signifies a 'forked antler,' from *uskwalgu*, antler,
but indicates that the antler is attached in place, as though the deer itself
were concealed below."

So a great deer breathes here, concealed in this mountain pass,
which may explain the fog wreathed on these slopes in early spring.
Uskwalgu. Duni'skwalgun'i. Such words seem made of fractured rock,
each edgy syllable taken directly from nature, just as the name of the
wolf derived from the broken sound that rises and cracks on the air
above where wolves have gathered. An unseen wolf can make itself
suddenly present by howling its name. The stone deer comes into view
silently, like a deer you are hunting, a telltale part of it exposed by the
same slow time that uncovered these mountains, the complete form

of the animal visible only to those who understand the connotations of the shapes of things and who are able to see the antlers wreathed in these chill mists. There is either a great stone animal here or a mountain of flesh and bone. Perhaps both—in the old time, words and things were fused. In mythology, as in geology, form derives from metamorphosis.

This is to try to think like running water, a logic as hard to follow as a Cherokee walking cross-country in these woods. But the great stone antlers clearly center everything around them, and, as Mooney's etymology suggests, there is more here than meets the eye. I'm not Cherokee, and I have to think about these things before I can see them. But I knew from the start that those dark rock spires above the West Prong of the Little Pigeon River weren't chimneys, as they are now called, that they were, like wolves, the shape of something wild.

From the north, they are the broken and worn nubs of antlers only, a pronounced notch at the end of a ridge that comes to an abrupt end. The right beam has a small basal tine, the left is acorned and stumplike. Perhaps this is to look for the wrong thing, to be too literal. The burr of each antler is hidden in vegetation, the mountainous deer itself camouflaged by forest. Ravens hang in the air like eyes. The deer faces west, following the river at its feet toward *Usunhi'yi*, the Darkening Land, "where it is always getting dark, as at twilight." A broad-shouldered mountain hunts behind it. *Kana'ti*.

Hunter and hunted are made of the same stuff. The hunter would have the advantage in the morning, with the light behind him. In the evening, he would be blinded by the setting sun. The hunter is skillful and patient, but the prevailing wind in this mountain pass favors the deer, which is characteristically wary. Their virtues are balanced and the gap between them never narrows.

That a great deer is buried up to its stone eyes here—its nostrils filled with mountain laurel, flanks sheathed in spruce, belly tickled by hemlock, sandstone hocks and hoofs wet in the river—does not surprise me. It would be odd if the earth were empty.

As you scan this abrupt horizon, two images repeatedly meet the eye: the upward sweep of conifers, the sloping boughs of which reiterate the steep pitch of the mountainsides, and the spills of massive wedge failures sloughing rock in great piles, as if the mountains were shedding skin.

Nowhere in the Cherokee mountains is the relief of the landscape so pronounced. The relation of earth and sky is as precipitous here as falcon flight. The great mass of the southern Appalachian summit rises around *Duni'skwalgun'i,* a colloquy of six thousand–foot ridges mantled in red spruce and Fraser fir, the latter a crowning anomaly in a landscape full of botanical mysteries, a southern endemic that appears in only the most boreal conditions, a colder thing than spruce even.

A dark pelage of now-blighted Fraser fir was once the strongest sign of the accomplishment of the earth here, present to remind you, even from a distance, that the effect of mountains was to sort things out, to narrow and heighten the world to rare expressions of place. Full of the drama of making his way up the bare, glaciated flanks of Katahdin in 1846, Thoreau exclaimed that "the tops of mountains are among the unfinished parts of the globe." But here in the southern Appalachians, which in our time do not reach above tree line, the work seems done. The spirit of this place resides not so much in the romantic sweep of the horizon as in the fine grain of things underfoot, the variety and tenacity of life rooted in rock withdrawing beneath it.

The dominance of summit evergreens is one of the visual pleasures of fall, during which the shape and extent of their occupation of the mountains above four thousand feet slowly becomes distinct. They save the highest peaks from the barren, grizzled look of the lower slopes and, from a distance, seem to wax healthier through winter, as if they thickened in the cold like fur, emerging in their best hues after the first snowfall when an alpine ground light darkens them.

The vertical tension in this landscape is most pronounced in the dead of winter, when those dark conifers wait in an empty, hoarfrosted realm ripped by bitter summit winds. Most birds and mammals have scattered to better places. Deciduous forms of plant life have retreated within themselves. But spruce and fir play by rougher rules. Conifers are well past their evolutionary prime, but the old habits that allowed them to thrive in the Permian, when the Appalachians were forming, still serve them well in the Holocene. On difficult terrain and in difficult weather, their sturdy seeds and armored cones—a hardy, patient reproductive mechanism—are well suited to wait out harsh conditions that keep the deciduous trees of the lower slopes at bay. So the spruce and struggling fir wait out winter, wind-bent and desiccated, until the short, hard season falls apart in spring and they emerge, haggard as bears.

In Cherokee thought, the primary test of creation was constancy—wakefulness through the night for animals, wakefulness through winter for plants. The most ancient Cherokee understood what ecologists now call deep time and that life was sculpted into the most fantastic shapes by the most fundamental conditions. Darkness and cold, night and winter, were the great challenges:

> When the animals and plants were first made—we do not know by whom— they were told to watch and keep awake for seven nights, just as young men now fast and keep awake when they pray to their medicine. They tried to do this, and nearly all were awake through the first night, but the next night several dropped off to sleep, and the third night others were asleep, and then others, until, on the seventh night, of all the animals, only the owl, the panther, and one or two more were still awake. To these were given the power to see and to go about in the dark, and to make prey of the birds and animals which must sleep at night. Of the trees only the cedar, the pine, the spruce, the holly, and the laurel were awake to the end, and to them it was given to be always green and to be greatest for medicine.

And so the significance of evergreens, which shelter life and encourage the spirit through all conditions, was recognized as the equal of predation. A stand of spruce or fir was as powerful in its own way as a panther or wolf. That the highest, most difficult places in these mountains should be the home of such things was not surprising.

Some things are best seen from a distance. But if you come here, come in winter or, like now, at the ragged, leading edge of spring, when rotting snow is piled in circles around the hemlock and spruce while the buds of hardwoods are ready to explode and the first bloodroot rise out of the hoar-frosted soil. Keep your eye on such things. Ignore the road, the parking lot, the signs that tell you nothing. If there is noise around you, pretend it is the sound of crows.

Wash your face in the Little Pigeon River above where the trail crosses and understand that men and women have made ablutions here for ten thousand years, that this was the way from the north across the mountains toward *Kitu'hwa* in war and peace, that this place was known to the Shawnee and the Iroquois and the Lenape in the days when men thought nothing of walking from the Great Lakes to the Gulf of Mexico. Dug into that silver water, your forearms will ache with the cold of all the winters here; you will feel in the bones of your hands what the roots of spruce and fir feel, what the fractured surface of the Anakeesta outcrops feel when nothing is here except the bear and the raven, the wolf and the owl.

Walk in the woods where you can, slowly and irregularly, like an animal. Pretend you are a bear. Stop often. Flip stones; move logs aside. Tilt your head to hear. Growl and sniff the air. Unfocus your eyes to see. Let your thoughts melt toward metaphor. Stop thinking in words. Embrace the old taxonomy, savoring what is animate and inanimate, what is flexible and stiff, what is long and what is short, what is liquid and solid, what is round or unlike anything else. Enjoy the broadness of life so organized—the sanity of the tangible—and mark its details well. There is very little left of the original world, and the possibility of preserving what remains has passed. Nothing has escaped the contact. If the old Cherokee had not buried time itself here—had not seen and saved the great animals that live inside these mountains waiting for this troublesome interglacial to end—we would have nothing to look at and think about.

An overused, badly eroded trail climbs steeply to *Duni'skwalgun'i*, where at first you will see only crows wheeling in confusion over the rock, a weird cacophony that is part of things here. Wait. Spend time. The crows will depart. Moments, minutes—take anything you can get—sometimes a full hour of silence and solitude will appear miraculously, like sunlight on a chilly day.

Find an angle of repose in the rock, some commodious wrinkle of Pangaea smoothed by a quarter of a billion years of rain. Sleep. Slip into that fitful daytime dream state that wakes you with your own unease when your consciousness dives into the rock underneath you. Let it go— the earth diver in your mind. Dream dreams. See what you can find.

When you can't keep yourself from waking—it's too cold, or too warm—stand up and look around you, try to see what the great stone deer sees.

Late March hammers at winter with gusts that thrum this foot-worn peninsula of rock, a copperous outcrop fragmented into great scales tilted at an ancient angle of impact. This is Anakeesta, a Cherokee word of uncertain meaning (possibly "place of fir"), now the designation for this dark embodiment of metamorphosed slates and siltstones that you see also to the north and west, where worn canines and carnassials of this violently folded rock stand out against the sand-stone mass of the Unakas.

As the toothy Anakeesta ridges fall apart before your eyes, slowly crumbling as they shred clouds, ravens hang in the air below you, their broad wings beating, as if to warm the unsupportive air, their stony voices full of discontent. The flight play of ravens is serious, the exercise of war birds. When the sun has warmed *Duni'skwalgun'i*, the ravens swing back and forth across weak thermals, pitched down for speed, primaries spread so each can wheel at will, not sleekly like a falcon but abruptly with a violent change of heart, a warrior's deliberate exchange of balance for momentum in an unexpected direction. When two ravens close, for practice, they beat each other with their wings, falling together until one breaks off. Attacks in flight are frank and bold, the attackers giving themselves away with joyous cries as they dive to count coup on the ruffled necks of their comrades. This is the play of wolves taken to the air, and after you have watched the ravens of *Duni'skwalgun'i*, you will understand why, among the Cherokee, the great black bird is the highest rank of warrior, above even the wolf.

The gusting wind that buffets ravens doesn't ruffle anything else. The dwarf heaths of the outcrop have been pruned by winter into rigid thickets that have no more give in them than the rocks to which they cling. The waxy vanes of the *Ericaceae* gather sunlight so intently they do not flinch in the wind. The stout presence of Catawba rhododendron, perhaps the hardiest of the heaths, an indigenous picket in these high rocky places, is far more interesting in extremis than in bloom, when its prissy suburban flowers draw crowds. The thick-leaved evergreen takes whatever ground the conifers and hardwoods leave it, and so marks out difficult places and grows with difficulty, an austere talent that allows it to thrive between rock and air. It becomes as difficult as its terrain and marks the most impenetrable places in these mountains. This beautiful creature is all root and branch, twisted by every ray of sunlight that has come near it, bark shredded by the wind into the fringes of the war shirt. Over centuries, it will make soil underneath itself, aided by wedges of ice that worry the rock apart every winter and by the maze of mosses and lichens that occupy the shade beneath its whorled leaves.

On sunny days, mayflies rise with such enthusiasm out of the chill water of the Little Pigeon River, two thousand feet below, that they end up lost on this mountainside. Anakeesta is laced with iron sulfide that gives it a rusty sheen, which attracts the wayward insects. I've seen them dance over this outcrop at midday, egg-tipped abdomens extended down toward the still flows of rippled rock, which they misperceive as moving water. I've never seen a mayfly release its egg sack to the rock, but once attracted to it, they cannot easily break away, so they rise and fall persistently over the still red river, probing gingerly beneath them, lost in the internal logic of their art, mesmerized by the mountain.

Beyond the rusty rock underfoot, the lost genius of these mayflies, and the sturdy guard of the *Ericaceae*, the larger world lies around you, folded and eroded, an intercalation of sea sediments and odd, igneous intrusions propped against basement rock half as old as the earth. The entire landscape is stressed by faults that break against the grain of the longer inclinations of synclines and anticlines that take you back beyond "waves of mountains"—uncanny trope—to seas themselves.

Like language and earth, myth and science are roughly congruent here; the map of one may be laid on the map of the other, and the resulting patterns are mutually illuminating. The relief of facts is especially deepened by those myths that compress a view of nature that extends beyond its usefulness to man, a breadth of perspective that was and remains barely comprehensible in Western terms, a radical appreciation of the nature of things.

THOMAS RAIN CROWE

Sun Time

Here, at the end of what was once the Old Drover's Road, time stands almost still. Stands still in the sense that I am not living according to man-made time. Rather, I am living by the signs and the seasons. By the waxing and waning of the light- and heat-providing presence of the sun and moon. Zoro calls it "sun time." When he uses this phrase he means a life that is lived off the clock. A reality guided by nature alone. A "calendar" determined and dictated by seasonal cycles that become ingrained, encoded, and therefore instinctual with each passing "year" of experience in the wild, of the wild work.

Not only am I off the clock, but I am also off the grid. No electric power, no fluorescent light—nothing from the outside to which I am attached or obligated in terms of dependency or financial debt. Like the Amish, I have no power lines coming in off the road to my house. There are no radio or TV antennas disrupting the natural line of this landscape. There are no bills hidden in with the letters in my mailbox. This disconnected life, at times, feels like what it must feel like to free-fall through the air after jumping from a plane. What it must feel like to float weightless in space or ocean. It's a kind of physical and mental freedom that can't accurately be described with words. One has to have lived, I think, this antiumbilical experience to know the feeling of essentially being unplugged and culturally adrift.

With no clock or calendar in my cabin, I get up and go to bed with the sun. My body has become attuned to this pattern—so when the sun goes down every night, my body reacts and tiredness sets in and I am ready to sleep, and in the morning, when darkness is broken by the first rays of the sun, I'm wide awake—as if the sun were some kind of solar alarm clock. This goes on day after day, night after night, without change or failure.

It is similar with the seasons. I don't need to turn the pages of any calendar to know when it is spring. The birds, the butterflies, the blossoms on the trees and flowers, the greening of the grasses, the warming of the wind . . . all these things and more tell me of the arrival of the new season. The same is true in summer, fall, and winter. The signs make themselves evident and the mind and body take note and make the necessary adjustments. The body feels the shift and the mind begins thinking of corresponding seasonal things—like the exact day to go out under the apple trees to look for morels. While it doesn't hurt to know from years of observation that the return of the hummingbirds generally coincides with the appearance of this prince of the fungal world, the idea quite literally pops into the mind on the precise day that morel mushrooms will appear over in the orchard. Sounds uncanny, but this is how it works. I'll walk across Zoro's field to the pine trees and through the pines to the logging trail that goes up into the woods and beyond to the orchards, and beneath the limbertwigs, there they'll be! The whole process is automatic. Signals are triggered, neural-electric connections are made, and programmed thought patterns appear on the screen of the mind, getting me ready for the wild work ahead for that season, until the signs and the signals shift again in about three full moons.

I much prefer nature's clock to the other methods and devices of keeping time. I've only owned and worn a watch once in my life, and that was only for a few days as a teenager, having received a cheap wristwatch for a birthday present when I was fifteen. No sooner had I put it on than I began checking the time—almost incessantly, neurotically. Every few minutes, it seemed, I would twist my wrist or push up my sleeve and look at my watch. I remember always being aware of the time, to the point where it was an ever-present and ominous specter that hung over me everywhere I went and with everything I did. I remember feeling imprisoned by this device on my wrist and what it represented. It quickly became so all pervasive and preoccupying (even to the point where my fixation on time was keeping me from sleep) that I took off that watch and threw it away (much to the dissatisfaction of my parents). I've never worn or owned another watch since. Being a prisoner to time for those few days during my youth parallels my experiences in subsequent years when I worked in factories, plants, and other jobs that necessitated punching in at a time clock at the beginning and end of the workday. This sort of relationship with time made me feel like I was little more than a number, albeit a body, chained to a huge and ominous System to which I had become enslaved.

Here in the woods along the Green River, with no watches, clocks, or calendars, there is none of that feeling of enslavement. Rather, in direct opposition to that, there is a feeling of freedom, even flight. I am master of my time and my movements. I live entirely in the moment, rather than by the clock. The past, the present, and the future seem, somehow, part of the same space-time continuum. The present seems never ending and includes the past, taking it along for the ride like a companion or lifelong friend.

When I watch the wild turkeys that often wander into the garden field, they go about their business of searching for grain, foraging through the compost pile, pecking at the fall grapes low to the ground in the arbor, and just searching in general in a timeless fashion. They are not scurrying about as if at any moment a whistle will blow or a bell will ring to remind them of another deed that needs doing. Going about their business, they just *are* there in the field, at one with the field, their work, and the day. I can't help but laugh at the thought of my wild friends strutting around my garden field adorned with wristwatches, as if they were shopping at the supermarket before having to hurry off to pick up the kids at school. Fact is, that I find that I've become more like these turkeys than I am like the folks I run into in town, who rush about as if a pack of wolves were hot on their heels. Rarely comfortable where they are and doing what they are doing, they seem to be forever on edge and a little off balance—as everywhere, all around them and on their bodies, they are reminded of their obligations to the Great God of Time.

Here in this world away from blowing whistles, ringing bells, and ticking timepieces, I am, maybe, and ironically, more aware of time than those who live and are enslaved by it. In fact, I've found that when pressed by my infrequent and time-conscious visitors from the outside world as to what time it is, I can usually come within one or two minutes of the actual time—just from noticing the position of the sun in the sky or the length of shadows cast by trees or buildings on the ground. Or the temperature and the barometric pressure in the air. My visitors think this to be some sort of magic when performed, but, assuredly, it is not some sort of sleight-of-hand trick. Rather, it's just that my sensory system, my body, has become so finely and intuitively tuned that my response to time is automatic, autochthonous—much the same as a few remarkable musicians I've known who are sound-sensitive to pitch and can call out keys from hearing a single note.

Being in place (in with place) means being in the moment, of the moment. Living in the wild, in nature, I am truly in place. In this place there is only the moment. It is a long, slow moment, to be certain. But it's always there and I am always a part of it. And in this sense, I know where and who and when I am. There is no confusion. There is no uncertainty. There is no hesitation. There is no rush. There just is. And that is it. I am here. And the time is now. What else can there be?

Slow down!
Where are you going in such a rush?
To the supermarket of your last dime?
Is the sound of pencil lead on paper
too much for your ears?

At fifty miles per hour
the butterfly on the rose by the side of the road
is as invisible
as a wish for the answer to prayers.
As you run through your best years
watching the road.

Faster than the speed of life.

Air

JAN DEBLIEU

Into the Dragon's Mouth

It begins with a subtle stirring caused by sunlight falling on the vapors that swaddle the earth. It is fueled by extremes—the stifling warmth of the tropics, the bitter chill of the poles. Temperature changes set the system in motion: hot air drifts upward and, as it cools, slowly descends. Knots of high and low pressure gather strength or diminish, forming invisible peaks and valleys in the gaseous soup.

Gradually the vapors begin to swirl as if trapped in a simmering cauldron. Air molecules are caught by suction and sent flying. They slide across mountain ridges and begin the steep downward descent toward the barometric lows. As the world spins, it brushes them to one side but does not slow them.

Tumbling together, the particles of air become a huge, unstoppable current. Some of them rake the earth, tousling grasses and trees, slamming into mountains, pounding anything that stands in their way. They are a force unto themselves, a force that shapes the terrestrial and aquatic world. They bring us breath and hardship. They have become the wind.

I stand on a beach near sunset, squinting into the dragon's mouth of a gale. The wind pushes tears from the corners of my eyes across my temples. Ocean waves crest and break quickly, rolling onto the beach like tanks, churned to an ugly, frothy blue-brown. The storm is a typical northeaster, most common in spring but also likely to occur in January or June.

Where I live, on North Carolina's Outer Banks, the days are defined by wind. Without it the roar of the surf would fall silent; the ocean would become as languid as a lake. Trees would sprout wherever their seeds happened to fall, cresting the frontal dune, pushing a hundred feet up with spreading crowns. We would go about our lives in a vacuum. That is how it feels in the few moments when the wind dies: ominous, apocalyptic. As if the world has stopped turning.

I lounge on the beach with friends, enjoying a mild afternoon. A light west breeze lulls and then freshens from the east. Its salty tongue is cooling and delightful at first, but as the gusts build to fifteen miles an hour we begin to think of seeking cover. We linger awhile—how long can we hold out, really?—until grains of sand sting our cheeks and fly into our mouths. As we climb the dune that separates us from the parking lot, I am struck anew by the squatness of the landscape. Nothing within a half-mile of the ocean grows much higher than the dune line. Nothing can withstand the constant burning inflicted by maritime wind.

On this thread of soil that arches twenty miles east of the mainland, every tree and shrub must be adapted to living in wind laden with salt and ferociously strong. Gusts of fifty miles an hour or more will shatter any limbs that are less pliant than rubber. We have no protection from raw weather here; we are too far out to sea. There is nothing between the coast and the Appalachian Mountains, hundreds of miles inland, to brake the speed of building westerly breezes. There is nothing between the Outer Banks and Africa to dampen the force of easterly blows.

Any book on weather will tell you that winds are caused by the uneven heating of the earth. Pockets of warm and cold air jostle each other, create an airflow, and *voilà!* the wind begins to blow. Air moves from high pressure to low pressure, deflected to the right or the left by the rotation of the earth. It is a simple matter of physics. I try to keep that fact in mind as I stand on the beach, bent beneath the sheer force of air being thrown at me, my hair beating against my eyes. Somehow, out in the elements, the wisdom of science falls a bit short. It is easier to believe that wind is the roaring breath of a serpent who lives just over the horizon.

The wind, the wind. It has nearly as many names as moods: there are siroccos, Santa Anas, foehns, brickfielders, boras, williwaws, Chinooks, monsoons. It has, as well, unrivaled power to evoke comfort or suffering, bliss or despair, to bless with fortune, to tear apart empires, to alter lives. Few other forces have so universally shaped the diverse terrains and waters of the earth or the plants and animals scattered through them. Few other phenomena have exerted such profound influence on the history and psyche of humankind.

From the soft stirrings that rustle leaves and grasses on summer afternoons to the biting storms that threaten life and limb, wind touches us all every day of our lives. We pay homage to its presence or absence each time we dress to go outside. We worship it with sighs, curses, and tears. "She's blowin', she is," the captain of a commercial fishing boat told me one stormy day shortly after I moved to the Outer Banks. As I struggled to keep my footing on a salt-slicked dock, I had to agree. Thereafter I made the expression part of our household vernacular. "She's blowin', she is," my husband and I joked those first winters, as Arctic-born breezes set our teeth on edge. She is, she is. But what in God's name *is* she?

In strict scientific terms wind is scarcely more than a clockwork made up of gaseous components. The heat of the sun and the rotation of the earth set the system ticking and keep it wound. The gears are simply air's inherent tendency to rise when heated and fall when cooled.

These patterned movements of air fasten into place the bands of wind and calm that girdle our small globe. A belt of constant low pressure rings the earth's middle, a weather equator that creates a strip of general breezelessness popularly known as the doldrums. To the north and the south the moist breath of the trade winds stirs the atmospheric stew. The pleasant trade regions are bounded in the northern and southern hemispheres by the comparatively stagnant zones known as the horse latitudes—so named, legend holds, because calm air within them slowed the sailing ships of early explorers and forced crew members to conserve water by throwing horses overboard. A significant portion of the world's deserts lie within the horse latitudes. Above and below 35 degrees, in the two breezy zones that encompass most of North America, Europe, China, Argentina, Chile, and New Zealand, prevailing westerlies revive the flow. These give way to bands of light easterlies that encircle the farthest, coldest reaches of the earth.

The atmosphere's alternating punches are felt most solidly in the southern hemisphere, where large expanses of open ocean enable winds to gather serious power. In the northern hemisphere the major continents harbor standing cells of high pressure; the wind must weave its way between pressure cores and over land features—mountains, valleys, cities—that muddy its flow and retard its passage. But in the north, wind unleashes catastrophic strength in the form of tornadoes that shred entire towns and northeasters that set seas chopping at shorelines like ravenous beasts.

The two contrasting faces of wind—its predictability and its moodiness—imbue it with the qualities of an animate being. Like the human body, wind is much more than the simple sum of its parts. Cool, gentle breezes seem peculiarly designed to nurture and heal, while storms strike us as personifications of the wrath of God. "This is the disintegrating power of a great wind: it isolates one from one's kind," Joseph Conrad wrote in *Typhoon*. "An earthquake, a landslip, an avalanche, overtake a man incidentally, as it were—without passion. A furious gale attacks him like a personal enemy, tries to grasp his limbs, fastens upon his mind, seeks to rout his very spirit out of him."

Out in a tempest on a boat being tossed by angry seas, it is difficult to think of the wind as a passive player in deciding one's fate. Wind has served as the pivotal factor in many lives, and in the histories of many peoples. Early explorers, from the Polynesians to the Vikings to the Spaniards, were led by favorable breezes to follow certain routes. As a result, Brazil was settled by Europeans more than a century before the west coast of Africa was, and Cortés ravaged the Aztecs and dismantled their empire a hundred years before the Pilgrims landed at Plymouth Rock. Key battles have been won and entire armies vanquished because of fortuitous turns of wind.

I like to speculate about how the world might be different if wind had arranged itself in other patterns, defying physics. Which would be the richer nations and which the poorer? Where might the rain forests lie and the great deserts? What of the history of this country? In 1777 George Washington defeated Charles Cornwallis in a crucial battle that turned when a north wind froze muddy roads along the Delaware River and enabled the new Americans to quickly reposition their artillery. If not for that wind, might we still be subjects of a distant queen or king?

Between 35 and 36 degrees north latitude, the thin islands known as the Outer Banks lie in a band of spirited west wind that accelerates as it moves over the Piedmont region and toward the Atlantic Ocean. The weather of this coast is shaped by the westerlies that scream across the continent in winter, pushing calmer, milder air far south.

Offshore the wide, warm Gulf Stream ropes its way north past Cape Hatteras and turns back out to sea after a close swipe at land. It mingles briefly with the cold, dying tongues of the southbound Labrador Current. In terms of weather, the junction of these two flows is enough to stop the show. In winter, when a dome of high pressure from the Arctic drifts southeast, it may come to the edge of the Gulf Stream and stall.

Will it linger or be pushed over the Gulf Stream and out to sea? Suppose there is a core of warm air off the coast, just east of the Stream. At the same time, suppose the jet stream has grown unusually strong and is flowing toward the northeast. The two air masses bump against each other like huge bubbles, the cold air fighting to move east, the warm air prodded north by the jet stream. A pocket of turbulence develops in the crook between them. Wind flows east, then is bent quickly to the north. Unable to resist the centrifugal force, it begins to move full circle, creating a system of low pressure that deepens violently.

The barometer plummets; rain descends in torrents. Up north, snow falls thick and fast. The western edge of the Gulf Stream is where great winter storms are made. They drift north, bequeathing rain to the Outer Banks usually, but sometimes snow. And wind.

In the spring of 1962 an explosive low-pressure system developed unexpectedly over the Outer Banks. In the wake of fierce northeast winds, the ocean pounded the shore for three days, spilling over the dunes and through the little towns tucked behind them. During that particular meteorological episode, known as the Ash Wednesday Storm, people woke to find the ocean sloshing into their beds. This cycle of weather has been repeated many times since, though never with a force equal to that of the first.

Such sudden, lashing northeasters have always intrigued coastal forecasters, who as recently as the early 1980s were at a loss to explain them. Now, with the help of Doppler radar, satellite photographs, and computer models of the atmosphere, meteorologists can often tell when a winter low-pressure system threatens to form over the coast. They can warn island residents, with some confidence, to buckle down for a storm.

More typically the wind blows fickle, and its swings of mood are devilishly tricky to foretell. At the center of a pressure core the wind speed slows, but at the edges it quickens. A strong knot of high pressure, sliding over the coast, may bring light wind that lasts for days. The system may stall long enough to dissolve, or it may venture out to sea, stirring up gales as it passes.

How much wind tomorrow? Technicians at the weather station make their educated guesses, knowing all along that the wind may fool them. Knowing that whatever else it does, the wind will call the day's tune.

Before the advent of worldwide forecasting systems, islanders watched for subtle changes to predict the behavior of weather and wind. They studied the sky and the animals the way a mother might look for the telltale signs that her young child is growing tired and cross. If, in a light, variable wind the gulls stand facing north, watch for steady north wind by nightfall. If clouds form a halo around the moon, count the stars within the halo. If there are three, expect bad weather for the next three days.

A mackerel sky—one with clouds that look like fish scales—means rain is on the way. A sundog at sunset foretells a bad storm. A mild spell in December or January is a "weather breeder"; it brings penetrating cold before winter's end. "A warm Christmas," an elderly island man once told me, "makes a fat cemetery."

The intensity of the weather here always depends on the wind, and the traditional sayings impart more folk wisdom about gales and breezes than about any other facet of life. A heavy dew in the morning means heavy wind by afternoon. If a swarm of biting flies shows up on a fishing boat far offshore, a land breeze is bound to shift to an ocean breeze. When the wind swings hard to the northeast, it will most likely blow itself out in a day:

A Saturday shift, come late or soon,
It seldom stands till Sunday noon.

Once or twice a winter, however, a northeaster lasts for most of a week. No matter how it begins or ends, local lore holds that the blow will always diminish on the third, or fifth, or seventh day, never on the second, fourth, or sixth day.

Only fools lived at the edge of the ocean back before hurricanes could be spotted on radar. The houses of Outer Banks natives nestled together in wooded sections just off Albemarle and Pamlico sounds. The sound side was considered the front of the islands, and the ocean beach, where the fury of storms hit hardest, was thought of as the back. It was the jumping-off point, the place where daring souls—swimmers, sailors, fishermen—could venture from the encircling arms of a continent into an ocean of uncertainty and terror. Islanders spoke of their homeland as if they were intent on keeping their backs to the wind.

The cattle that ranged freely across the Outer Banks in the late nineteenth and the early twentieth century seemed to know when a weather shift was imminent, and they anticipated changes in the wind to escape biting flies. If they moved to the "back of the beach," east wind was on the way. If they migrated to the marshes, the easterly breeze would swing west. Most of the time the range stock stayed in the open grasslands and dunes. When they wandered into the villages, residents began boarding up windows for a hurricane.

Normally the wind migrates slowly from northeast to east to southeast to southwest, moving clockwise in the anticyclonic pattern typical of high-pressure systems in the northern hemisphere. There are exceptions, of course, when the wind direction shifts backward—counterclockwise. For generations native islanders have known such a pattern to be a harbinger of the most violent storms. The weather change might come as a localized thunderstorm or a devastating hurricane, but a backing wind is always to be feared. As an old saying has it, "I'd rather look at Grandma's drawers than see a backing wind."

Wind is culture and heritage on the Outer Banks; wind shapes earth, plant, animal, human. Wind toughens us, moves mountains of sand as we watch, makes it difficult to sleepwalk through life.

The spring I moved to the islands I lived in a house beset by wind. Air seeped easily through the decayed siding and whistled through the roof. The constant clatter made me lonely and chafed my nerves, but I gladly sought the shelter of those rooms rather than stand exposed to the chilling breeze. I developed a ritual for going out: before opening the door I pulled on my coat and gloves, yanked down my hat, and braced myself for an onslaught. I conditioned myself slowly, taking walks in steady wind for twenty minutes at first, with the hope of working up to forty-five. An appreciation for wind was not in my nature; I had to learn to like the feel of air pummeling my chest and roaring across my skin. "Light" wind, I learned, blew less than fifteen miles an hour. Anything less than ten miles an hour was not worthy of mention.

Walking with my hood pulled hard against my scalp, I began to notice how animals coped with wind. Terns, the kamikazes of the bird world, seemed oblivious even to hard gales. I remember watching them one spring afternoon at Oregon Inlet as air howled down on us from the north and waves sloshed against each other. Together wind and tide made a mess of the landscape; with the frothing water and the whipping branches of wax myrtle shrubs, it seemed as if the world were being shaken to its foundations. Yet the terns hung steady in midair, flapping their wings quickly and chittering to each other, their beaks pointed downward as they scanned the ocean for fish.

Not many animals come out in such wind. Those that do may find the normal parameters of life redrawn. In a sustained east wind the water in the sounds is pushed toward the mainland so that vast stretches of sandy bottom are exposed. Islanders refer to this as the tide running out, and indeed it is the only kind of falling tide to be seen on the banks' western shore. The water level in the estuaries here does not respond to the pull of the moon. All sound tides are erratic and driven strictly by wind; they ebb in northeasters and flow during westerlies.

Soon after I moved here I learned that water swept east by wind for many miles has a way of suddenly spilling over its normal banks, like a bowl tipped sloppily to one side. One morning after several days of hard west wind, I parked in a lot near a fish house on Pamlico Sound. An islander casually warned me, "You might ought to move your car, case we get some tide." I parked on higher ground. Within an hour three feet of briny water covered the fish-house lot.

Even the more docile winds affect the shape of the water and the distribution of creatures within it. East winds send the surf pounding against the beach; west winds slow the shoreward roll of breakers and make them stand erect. The best surfing waves are sculpted by a northeast blow that shifts cleanly to the west. But if the west wind blows too long, the breakers are knocked flat. Surfers disappear, replaced by commercial fishermen, who row dories just offshore to set their nets for bluefish and trout.

We all have our favorite winds. Outer Banks surf casters like a land breeze because, as they say,

> Wind from the east, fish bite the least.
> Wind from the west, fish bite the best.

A westerly breeze draws trout, mullet, and other species to the calm waters in the lee of the shore. During duck hunting season it also pushes waterfowl from the middle of Pamlico Sound toward the islands, putting them in easy range of hunting blinds. A friend of mine, an avid hunter and fisherman who lives on Hatteras Island, grew so enamored of the sound-side breeze that he vowed to name his firstborn son West Wind. His wife's wisdom prevailed; they named the child Teal.

Good fishing or poor, the light summer easterlies are dearest to my heart. West winds muddy the ocean waters, but east winds clear them. West winds bring biting flies to the beach, but east winds banish them to the marsh. The most pleasant summer days are those with an ocean breeze strong enough to set up a little surf but not so strong as to make swimming dangerous. Waves roll lazily ashore as wind gently fills my lungs, caresses my skin, and sweeps cobwebs from my brain. I lie in the sun, hot but cool enough for reading. I slip noiselessly into the clear green surf and float on top, watching as sparkling grains of sand tumble out to sea between waves.

I live in an island forest now, where tree trunks slash the winter wind before it can hit the house full force. At night I listen to the loblolly pines pitching back and forth high overhead and wonder how many more years the cottages on the ocean will be able to stand against the forces that batter them.

At times I imagine that the wind takes on different personas, like a god that is capable of assuming any living form. I still often think of it as the breath of a dragon, though it usually feels more like ice than fire. Its gustiness, its ability to surround and overpower me, seem to be of mythical greatness; yet it is undeniably real. I do not bundle up as carefully as I used to when I go out; to tell the truth, I now look forward to the cleansing power of heavy blows. But unlike the old-timers, I will never think of the ocean as the back side of the islands. It is the front line of battle, the front line against the wind.

Over the past dozen years I have been in perhaps a hundred windstorms here. A few have stayed in my thoughts. One of my clearest memories is of an August day when I stood on the back porch of my little wind-haunted house and waited for a hurricane to roar through.

It was 1986, the year of Hurricane Charley—a runt, as hurricanes go, but with gusts to eighty-five miles an hour. A friend had come over to visit my husband and me with his dog, a Chesapeake Bay retriever. The storm, passing offshore, was throwing off east wind and was not expected to do much damage. Even so, no one wanted to be out in it. It was enough to stand on the leeward side of the house and watch the myrtle bushes being shaken like rag mops.

That summer a pair of Carolina wrens had built a nest in the pump house and raised several broods. There were still chicks in the nest when the storm hit. In the excitement I had forgotten about the wrens, when I saw a quick movement under the dilapidated table where we cleaned fish.

An old beach chair was folded and propped beneath the table. Leaning over, I could see an adult wren clinging to the chair. He was soaked from rain and, judging from his hunched posture, too exhausted to move even as far as the pump house. He knew we had caught him off his home base, but he did not seem to care.

The others noticed the wren the same second I did. Nobody moved, not even the retriever, although he eyed the wren with a lazy spark of interest. Nobody did anything except look out at the wind and rain. We stood on the back porch, an unlikely alliance—two men, a woman, a dog, a bird—each of us snagged momentarily from the flow of our normal lives, refugees from the wind.

JANISSE RAY

Riding Bareback
through the Universe

The earth does not move steadily,
spinning at one moderate speed through the heavens,
but with the motion
of a wild stallion at full gallop
across a painted desert, toward a mesa.
Which is sweep and fall, glide and fall,
the lovely waltz of waves.
The tail of the earth streams behind like a comet,
its streak a dancing line.
So every heavenly body, once thought steady, even,
flings itself along filled with senseless joy,
an ecstatic herd leaping through the skies.
We ride standing
on the back of time itself, its nostrils
shooting fire—
side by side, our feet firmly planted,
we ride at full gallop,
our love for this life so thunderous and billowing,
so wild and powerful
we finally understand planetary movement
although we too had thought it more stoic.
Now around us thousands of leaves
leap up and down on their stems
and the heads of spring flowers
ride like falcons on the back of the wind.

Air

Before they learn to fly, flight is in their minds, some myth of *Archaeopteryx*. All morning they will stand at the cliff's edge and stare, as if trying to remember. For hours they preen themselves and wind-hover, until they let go of the world and suddenly there is no place on the jagged bedrock from which to follow how they twist the air.

At midday they are in the sun and the sky becomes a place where falcons were.

Toward evening, underwings gleaming, they return as scimitars, blades swept out of heaven, or as life weaving flight out of nothing— gliding, turning, soaring to stall on rising columns of air, then stooping, for practice, at the earth.

Eeseeoh. River of many cliffs. Halfway home, at Linville Gorge in North Carolina, where I often stop to watch for peregrine falcons.

Eeseeoh is a questionable tidbit I picked up from a field guide and does not look or sound like a Cherokee word. The corruption and loss of language, like the corruption and loss of land and wildlife, seems inescapable. My own struggle with understanding the past was full of errors and misconceptions, no doubt. Pursuing the truth in things head-on is ill-advised. But *Eeseeoh* signifies in its garbled way something about the nature of this place—there is, in fact, a cliff-shrouded river thousands of feet below me.

Historically, the Linville River gorge was known to be a Cherokee place. The dramatic skyline of its north rim is composed of sacred shapes—now known as Hawksbill and Table Rock—which can be seen from as far away as the Black Mountains, the strangest mountains in the Cherokee landscape and where *Kana'ti's* cave is said to be. The rock expressions at Linville Gorge are best observed from a distance. Get too close to them and you will see that they are desecrated, ruined with trash and trails, hardly seen or treated for what they are. At the head of the gorge there is a spectacular fall of water over rippled ledges of granite and gneiss, an unusual breach in Blue Ridge basement rock that lets the river flow east into a rectangular plunge pool that looks very much like the drawing of the elusive lake of the Cherokee on the Le Moyne map.

The Linville River often is heavily laden with silt from the overdeveloped land upstream, but despite plans in the nineteenth century to dam the river, it still flows freely, wild and loud. There are stands of old growth in the gorge, most of which is too steep to log profitably. Wildness takes care of its own when it can. Ancient eastern hemlock and monumental tulip poplar thrive in the cliffy river mist. Claire Newell did fieldwork here the summer before I met her in the Kilmer-Slickrock Wilderness. She reminded me that Andre Michaux had botanized at Linville Gorge in the late eighteenth century—looking for wonders among *"les roucers de al Montagne Hock-bill et de Table Montagn"*—and that the type description for *Pinus pungens*, table mountain pine, was made here by Michaux and honors, indirectly, the Cherokee claim to this landscape.

If the solemn, oriental eastern hemlock is my favorite forest tree, the rugged table mountain pine, a southern Appalachian endemic, is my favorite species of the edge. *Pinus pungens* thrives between rock and air, where no other tree could imagine itself. A table mountain pine grows here where I watch for falcons, with Hawksbill to the west and Table Rock itself to the east across the open space of the river gorge. Having broken through barren rim rock, the twisted pine occupies an empty place even the stunted mountain laurel nearby shun. But despite its difficult circumstances, the tree is heavily laden with clusters of its fiercely spined and tightly shut cones.

Although compared to forest hardwoods it is not an especially long-lived tree, the thick-skinned table mountain pine tends to keep hold of the difficult sites it occupies. The species' persistence in the same place from generation to generation was not lost on the Cherokee, for whom the tree was a symbol of long life and health. The tree's relationship to fire, on which it thrived, undoubtedly did not go unnoticed. The jagged conifer was shaped like lightning and loved high-elevation rock outcrops where lightning frequently struck. Fire suppressed *Pinus pungens'* few competitors and opened its brutal cones, which could stay closed for as long as a quarter of a century. The undistinguished-looking pine needed fire as much as water to survive.

Like the table mountain pine and the red wolf, the peregrine falcons for which I wait on this late-summer evening are also part of myth and history. As an airborne predator the peregrine has no equal, not even among the eagles. Long ago, the idea of the peregrine had become the Thunderbird of the Southeastern Ceremonial Complex and had enlarged itself into the dreaded *Tla'nuwa'*, the great hawk of the Cherokee imagination. If the wolf was the finest reification of the wildness of animals, the slender but ferocious peregrine falcon was the final form of what has been called the "evolutionary triumph" of flight.

Historically, however, the peregrine's fate had been much like that of the red wolf. The combined ill effects of pesticides and loss of nesting sites decimated the species in the eastern United States during the twentieth century. An extensive search of all known historical aeries in 1964 found them empty; in fact, the eastern subspecies of peregrine—the Appalachian peregrine—was extinct. Beginning in the 1970s, a closely related subspecies was reintroduced in the Appalachian and Adirondack mountains and along the Atlantic coast. Before I had even heard of the red wolf, I spent two summers watching the hacking of peregrine falcons from a cliff in the Blue Ridge Mountains of Virginia.

The release of falcons to the sky is as undramatic as the release of wolves to the earth. Young birds are trucked and carried to a suitably remote cliff site in plywood boxes, one side of which is screened so that they can acclimate themselves to their new location. The birds are fed quail and pigeons and watered by hack site attendants they never see, who protect them from foxes and raccoons. After a few days, the screening is removed from the hack boxes and the birds emerge. Their first response to this unprecedented freedom, this strange reprieve from history, is to be stunned and cautious. For days you can observe the most agile bird on earth, the fastest animal alive, walking about apparently unaware, or unsure, of its great skills. The beautiful birds shift their scaly feet nervously on the slanting rock, looking down at it, and shuffle their wings about as if their wings were in the way. Until they fly, they must view the space before them as we do, as empty and dangerous.

The instinct to fly is no doubt inborn, but the young falcons are per-haps encouraged by the silent turkey vultures passively riding ther-mals rising from the valley floor and by the ravens that frequently come to play loudly in the air in front of the cliff. The flight of a raven is clearly an improvement on the flight of the vulture, but falcon flight is another thing entirely and the mockery—or the challenge—of ravens eventually becomes too much for falcons to bear.

After a day or two, the young falcons begin taking short glides into the treetops below them, getting a feel for the lift in their shapely wings, the powers of their form. They make short flights back and forth in front of the hack site, swinging farther out of view each time. After they learn to hitch rides on midday thermals, which take them to new heights and load their wings with possibilities the vultures and ravens cannot imagine, they begin to exercise the freedom of their wildness and create a fabulous order in the air no one would have imagined without them.

Like newly released wolves, the peregrines return for a few weeks to their release point, practicing the art of flight in a familiar place. I remember spending days at the hack site watching the sky—the shock of their sudden appearance from impossible angles, their balletic flight, and then the way they were suddenly gone, at first for hours, and then for days. Once they have fully explored their extraordinary maneuverability, and fitted it to hunting moths, butterflies, and birds, falcons stoop less and less frequently past the hack site and even their distant cries are heard less often. They learn to disdain the food left for them. One by one they disappear forever. In a month or so they are gone. Some wildness has disappeared back into the world and the work is done. After lingering for a few weeks, to make sure the birds are gone, the hack site attendants take the memory of falcons, visible and invisible, home with them.

The bedrock truth of Romanticism, resistant to even the most cor-rosive modernism, is that consciousness is our participation in the infinite. But consciousness needs found objects—the wolf, the falcon, the table mountain pine. Our only access to the infinite is through nature, where we find, coldly bordering our own mortality, all time and all space—the shifting geography of being expressed through the art of evolution. To see a falcon or a wolf, or an eastern hemlock or a table mountain pine, and suddenly understand something about yourself or your culture is not necessarily to anthropomorphize.

I saw red wolves in the backcountry once, for a minute or two. I have never seen or heard a peregrine falcon except at a hack site. Still, having seen the wolf and the falcon, I can now imagine them and pursue, from a distance, the truth and beauty I know for a fact they embody. I would not want to do without either the fact or the image, and I do not understand a culture that willfully destroys its access to such things. For whatever reason.

"Thus the animal lives unhistorically," Nietzsche writes, sounding oddly like Thoreau, "it hides nothing and coincides at all moments exactly with what it is; it is bound to be truthful at all times, unable to be anything else." It seems that we cannot escape what Albert Camus, hardly a Romantic, called the "innocence of the wolf"—a wildness some love and some hate. Whatever it is, the wildness hits close to home.

Of course, animals don't live unhistorically. The falcons banded and released those two summers in the Blue Ridge nested in Pittsburgh and New York because in the East there is more cliff space on skyscrapers than in the mountains, where tracts of homes crawl up the slopes everywhere, everyone jostling for a slightly better view of what their own presence destroys. And the red wolves of the southern Appalachians were hemmed in, as I was, by pollution and roads and the ugly boom towns of rural tourism, which also destroy their own reason for being.

But Nietzsche put his finger on the philosophical essence of wildness—a truthful, sacred being in animals that slips through history where it can and that we admire even though the history that destroys the truth and beauty we desire is our own.

ANN FISHER-WIRTH

Of

When the soul is tired and full of grief
the hands must continue to live
honorably,
feeling the dog's thick ruff or the tender crease of his armpits
for plump summer ticks, plucking them, creasing them
between fingernails, and then the blood spurt.

Poetry is of the hands, how they caress and care
for the hot, itch-plagued animal,
while the soul
wanders vacant all day long
where bald cypresses grip down in muck,
loom up through the snakethick, shadowfevered river.

SUSAN CERULEAN

Origin Moment

I hold in my hand a fragment of ancient pottery, remembering the winter day when I plucked it from the lip of a low tide. It is just a shard, shaped like the point of a spear, the length of my smallest finger. One side is smooth and dark, the other cast red by the clay from which it was fashioned more than two thousand years ago. Two sets of parallel lines at right angles to one another hint at the potter's intricate design. A third direction is established by a single line plunging toward the pieces that once linked my fragment into an intact vessel.

I will never see the pot that once held my shard or know anything of the artist who formed it with her hands. Still, as I study this fragment and go about my life in the red clay hills of north Florida where another woman excavated that clay for her art and her life, I feel deeply drawn toward what once was whole.

I want to understand that wholeness.

And so, I write about fragmentation and wholeness, about a bird's existence, and a woman's life. My story is a call for wholeness beyond what is offered by contemporary culture, more than what is postulated by science and reason, and different from the shape of the self-absorbed life I lived in the upper-middle class of North America in the second half of the twentieth century.

It is a story that I believe my grandmothers wished to tell me, although they could not. It is a story I am slowly piecing together from the potsherds of my own life and the lives of my people, beginning with the day I first yearned with my whole being after a certain living bird, the swallow-tailed kite.

Perhaps you have seen this wonderfully adroit flier, stark black and white, living origami, drifting over a wild southern river, using its deep forked tail as a sensitive rudder. Kites are hard to keep in sight or follow very far. If you have been lucky enough to spot one, you probably hope to repeat the experience.

Perhaps, as well, you have felt at your core a deep, unnamable longing, a wild hunger, which does not seem to correspond with the privileges and abundance of your life, and which sometimes drives you to do or consume things you'd rather you hadn't. Maybe the elements of fragmentation I have identified in my own life will resonate for many others in my culture, especially middle-class women, at this time on the planet. And allow us to move forward. For this journey is about wholeness, the intact verb of life, the swing of a planet and its belly-round moon, the response of a rare bird, and the holding of it all whole. My hope is that in the telling, the healing may begin.

The integrity of life on our tender emerald planet is so greatly at risk. We stand, as Thomas Berry tells us, at the end of the Cenozoic age, the great flowering age of plant and animal diversity. Our own species must stare full face at the annihilation we are inflicting. I wonder about the fault lines in our own culture. What are the fractured places in our hearts and minds and spirits that have allowed us to stand by and watch and even to participate in the destruction of so much of life? How might we invoke transformative powers, very different from those that appear to rule our world just now? I believe that is what we must do to revise our assault on the planet—take our proper place, a sustainable place, among all the other living things.

It was over the Edisto River in South Carolina that I saw my first swallow-tailed kite. My memory is etched with a clear image of how that bird swung into view and hung over me, suspended like an angel, so starkly black and white, with its wide scissored split of a tail. I rushed to grab binoculars, to take a closer look, almost flipping the canoe. The bird drifted on a breeze too subtle to sense, its breast a center point for the sleek maneuver of wing and tail, as if a kite string actually were attached to the deeply muscled breastbone. As suddenly as it appeared, the bird was gone.

If my grandmothers had still been alive all those years ago, when that first kite wheeled over the sunny run of the river, they might have translated for me the unfamiliar, inexpressibly powerful sensation I felt in my body. They might have told me this was the origin moment of my relationship with that rare and beautiful bird and the beginning of my own journey toward wholeness—not only for myself, but also on behalf of my mother, my grandmothers, and my unborn children (for I was only twenty-three years old at the time), and most important, for the living mantle of our beautiful and imperiled planet.

Even though my grandmothers were not there to interpret when the fleet kite shadow first darkened my face, I knew that something essential had come into my life, connecting me viscerally to wildness. I wanted that wildness. I wanted to leap out of the boat, to scramble over the abrupt knees of the cypress, and climb the insufficient wild aster vines. I wanted to follow that bird.

Only now do I begin to have words for what I felt, half-crouched within the aluminum confines of the silver canoe. I begin to name the wild desire that strained my body toward that awesome bird—and away from confinement in a curiously invisible prison I had never before recognized. I can begin to say how, in that swamp, my life fell into the world of the swallow-tailed kite, an unexpected gift from some god.

If I had returned home from my outing, marveling over the encounter with the swallow-tailed kite, and called to my grandmothers, and if they had been alive and whole, they would have helped me polish that river-bird-moment like a talisman, like the precious and portentous thing that it was. As we stood side by side at the double kitchen sink, rinsing the dinner forks, hips brushing, the steam from the soapy dishwater warming our faces, we would have talked through what I had seen and felt. We would have compared the kite to others on my life list of birds and remembered dreams one or the other of us had had of birds. My nana Lucille might have recalled how, as a small girl, I had raised an oriole nestling. My mother would have reminded us how I had loved to sit with my father and leaf through an encyclopedia of birds, how he would let me choose a bird sticker to lick and how firmly I would press the image of a redstart or a white pelican onto the page to mark that we had read and understood. My grandmother Alice would have remembered that my great-great-grandfather Jacob Isleib had been known as a fancier of wild birds back in

Prussia, an almost unknown pursuit in the mid-1800s. I would have felt my lineage running through me like a river.

At bedtime, we would have left the questions unanswered but still formed, like the rough outline in clay of a woman's full body, her breasts and her belly: How does this bird relate to our granddaughter's work in the world? What is that she is here to do, what is it that she must pursue with her whole life energy, while she is here on the planet? And those questions would have become our prayers. After the light in my room had been turned out, as I lay in the moments before sleep, turning the powerful impression of the day over and over in my heart, I would know that in their private rooms, my grandmothers were holding my journey in their hearts, too. That in the light of candles on the small altars on their cedar chests, prayers of gratitude and intercession were following the flame-smoke into the night air, seeking currents to carry them to the roosting place of the wild bird and to the heart of the wild planet itself. In this way my unfolding life would have been braided into the stories of my people. I would have come more quickly to know my place, the threads of responsibility that were mine to pick up and weave, the healing that I was to undertake: what I was here in this life to do. And if this had happened, my journey to the present might have been less clumsy, less circuitous, less hurtful to other people, for I would have understood early on the true nature of the wild hunger that lit my body that day and how to feed it more skillfully, accurately, appropriately. I would not have tipped so many lives into the black water, nor left so many homes, nor broken so many vows, no matter if they were taken in unguided ignorance.

But I am just groping my way into the wholeness that my grandmothers wished me to know and could not claim during their own turns at living. Due to the early deaths and emotional woundings of my elders, I am only beginning to cobble together our story, as well as my life, as best I can. I am sad that it has taken me so long and that my mother and aunts and grandmothers are not here with me, today, that we were not able to live longer and deeper in our physical lives together.

Among the Dagara tribe of west Africa, it is believed that children yet unborn, approaching their time in the fastness of their mothers' wombs, know their purpose in the world. In a ritual hearing conducted during the mother's pregnancy, in community, a shaman asks the child-who-is-to-come, "Tell us why you have been sent, your purpose for visiting us." Through the voice of its mother, who is in a trance, the child replies to the shaman and other family members. The grandfathers of the child name him or her accordingly and later act as confidante and guide, helping the young one assume the life program he or she indicated to the elders while still in utero.

Among my people, the northern Europeans translocated to the North American continent during the last two hundred years, another way used to be given to the growing child to help her know her path: the tending of her own origin moment. The origin moment is the split second early in life when memory takes hold in the body and the full presence of the young one's spirit as well. For us, our human origin moment is the instant when our baserock, permanent images, and assumptions begin to form as the planet becomes aware of itself through this new being, as it never has before. Wherever that child is located, all that she remembers, is her origin moment, and she will live her life forward from this moment of convergence, with whatever emotional overtones and cultural assumptions are included.

Among my people, this occasion customarily happens between the ages of one and two. In years past, the origin moment probably could be traced back much earlier, but our lives have constricted in matters of the old spirit ways. And in fact, when the child's caretakers or circumstances are harsher, or where there is extreme deprivation, or physical abuse, the moment of origin may come much later.

These origin moments set the course of the lives of the wild animals, as well as ourselves, and it is not so difficult to understand how the wind in the thin tops of tall pine trees informs even the embryos of swallow-tailed kite chicks in the egg and why they forever return to such fragile circumstances to build their own nests as adults.

In my own origin moment, my earliest memory, I stood alone in a crib, my hands gripping a smooth wooden rail, in a warm and darkened house. Outside a window, miles down and away to the southeast, blazed the brilliant electric lights of New York City. Between me and Manhattan Island, where my father went to work each day, I sensed the dark marshlands, the second-growth foothill forests and the dimmed stars. I fell into my human awareness from this place of watching. Behind me, although I was just barely over a year old, slept my baby sister in a second crib. Beyond her bed was the closed door to my parents' bedroom. There is a sense of neutrality and self-containment to my origin moment, a cast of loneliness. I did not bring together the knowing part of me, my human consciousness, in the arms of a parent, or within a circle of kin.

At the time memory and spirit recognized one another in the small child of my body, in the early 1950s in northern New Jersey, no swallow-tailed kites were anywhere nearby. It must have been January when I stood in my crib looking to the southeast, and it was dark outside, and kites do not often fly after dark, or in the winter cold. What I knew instead was the frosty outbreath of northern Appalachian trees, the special air they exhaled, and the way the snow melts on the south side of those trees and how cold shadows protect the snow on the northern exposure, striping the hillside white longer into spring than seemed bearable, especially for a (once again) pregnant mother of two very young children, such as my own mother. I knew that early winter darkness and the long spaces of the minutes between the drop of the dark and the hour when my father's train would return him home from New York City. Without even a word, my mother taught me this about time, how it is elastic, like the potential range of a bird, and how it can drown you, or bring you quickly to your heart's dearest dreaming.

So I would not have seen the swallow-tailed kite at the time of my origin moment. The spring delivered robins in May (not the winter redbreasts that flock to the native hollies where I live now in north Florida), but never a kite. I am certain I spent a lot of time watching those robins, for my Aunt Judy told me only last year that I was the kind of baby who could absorb herself with a single leaf fallen into her playpen for thirty minutes or more at a time. In any case, I came to love the birds, although not at first any more than all of nature, especially the sea. Perhaps I wasn't so hungry back then, for I do not remember feeling desperate to crawl after those ground-hopping robins or feverish longing as I did when, paddling a silver canoe, I saw my first kite at age twenty-three.

I'm thinking now that if my grandmothers had been with me at the time of my first origin moment—the fullness of who they really were, that is, not how they were actually able to interact with us when they were alive—those two hours in the dark before my father finally brought the excited and exhausted air of New York City into our kitchen would have been the time to tell this story.

Fire

CHRISTOPHER CAMUTO

Fire in the Path

> The wolves, which are not like those in Germany, Poland and
> Lapland (because they fear men and do not easily come near)
> give us such music of six different cornets, the like of which I
> have never heard in all my life. Several brethren, skilled in
> hunting, will be required to exterminate panthers, wolves, etc.
>
> THE MORAVIAN BISHOP SPANGENBERG,
> entering the Cherokee country in autumn of 1752

Above *Tsiya'hi*, to the south, the main ridge of the Unakas runs
southwest to northeast, part of that crest of Precambrian stonework
buried in the ground from Georgia to Newfoundland and uplifted in
the Permian, long before the earth thought of wolves. Two hundred
fifty million years of percussion have given the southern Appalachian
summit that monumental if weathered look we vaguely associate with
permanence but that we know, on reflection, is the shape of change.
These mountains revealed themselves by eroding and continue to
come into being, like wolves, in the act of disappearing.

In early November, mountains and wolves did in fact disappear into
the weather, moving behind the blind of raw, squally days that drives
visitors from roads and leaves the backcountry in relative peace for half
the year. If you watch them closely, day after day, the mountains take on
an added nobility in late fall, an effect both of longer shadows cast into
the lower slopes and hazeless air bathing their summits. The relief of the
landscape deepens, as if the grain of the underlying rock had tightened.
The shape of each ridge becomes more distinct, and the idea that these
mountains are ancient storehouses and council places for animals seems
not so fanciful. The grizzled pelage of the mountains in the middle dis-
tance may well be the flank of something sentient.

When, except for the tenacious oak and beech, the trees have shed
their leaves, longer views of the landscape open up, an invitation to

longer thoughts. Words emerge, each stark as a gray buck lifting its antlered head in bare timber to watch you, old signs with spirit of place in them.

Words for where you are and where you are going: *tsa'gi*, upstream, a way you often walk in the mountains, exploring, searching for a source; *ge'i*, downstream, the direction going home, the way not to be lost. *Nunna'hi*, for the path itself and, as it widens in space and time, the trail, the road. Words for patterns in the landscape that are also images: *gadalu'tsi*, fringe standing erect, the serried ranks of bare hardwoods on ridge crests you notice in the high country. This stark fringe relates the earth to the sky and filters the shifting light of shortening days. Looking west—*wude'ligun'yi*—at sunset, the trees are black and seem to move against the gold glow.

There were archaic, stony nouns for shapes in the land—*nugatsa'ni*, a high ridge with a long gradual slope—as well as for a man's passing or habitual relationship to that land—*gunun'dale'gi*, one who follows the ridge. And there were names for the agents of forest experience: the Homeric *nunyu'gunwani'ski*, for instance, rock that talks, which tells you the source of the voices you hear, that matter-of-fact, uncanny chatter that prompts dreams when you sleep by a stream in a forest. And now, once again, there was *wa'ya*, the howling of red wolves.

I was camped on Anthony Creek the first time I heard them, a few miles into the backcountry at a place where I started many a circular trek through wolf country. Opening my eyes before the second, longer note trailed off, I knew instantly what it was. I sat up in my sleeping bag and looked at my watch: 4:00 A.M. The wolf that woke me seemed to be across the stream and well above camp but clearly on my side of Anthony Ridge, a wedge that points toward the east end of Cades Cove, two or three miles downstream.

What woke me was a two-note ascending howl that lasted maybe three seconds. Perhaps there was more than one of these, the earlier phrases buried in my sleep. Then the wolf seemed to be moving about on the ridge, giving out test patterns of yips and barks with only an occasional howl. Twenty minutes of this. Then silence and sleep.

At 5:30, a wolf on that ridge again, very likely the same animal, giving a sustained howl, a bark rising to a howl, and another sustained howl.

All the same duration, about three seconds. I propped myself up on an elbow, groped for a notebook and pen, and stuck a small flashlight in my mouth. I made up a crude notation in which to record what I was hearing—the kind of sound and its relative duration: yip, yip, bark, pause, yip, yip, bark, the animal seeming to test or hold the dark air for itself. I thought it might be one of the juveniles trying to get the hang of a locator call. Then a set of strong, clear phrases pitched high enough to sound plaintive were there not so much apparent syntax in the vocalization: bark rising to the type howl, another such howl, then a howl descending to six barks and a bark rising to the two-note sustained howl.

After ten minutes of this, there was a response from downstream in a similar voice with more economy of phrasing: a bark rising to the sustained howl, bark rising to a shorter howl, another bark and the short howl.

Then the wolf on the ridge: bark rising to howl; bark, pause, bark, long pause, single note howl; then four widely spaced barks, a pause, and a final rising howl.

Two sustained rising howls rang out from the second wolf and reverberated into a silence that kept me awake until dawn. Not like anything else. Like *red wolves howling*.

I moved on the next morning, carried into a cold, blue November day buoyed by the cry and response of wolves. I doubt that we will ever understand the grammar of animals, the structure of consciousness that shapes their vocalizations. But open communication between two free-ranging wolves was, I thought, a mark of an improved world. This dialogue I had overheard and absurdly transcribed seemed a valuable addition to things.

The woods were bare now, the understory open and the canopy leafed only in daylight. But the leaves on the ground had not yet faded and gave the impression of bright paths leading everywhere. On the trail, the effect was of a snakeskin, imbrication of copperhead or timber rattler rendered in scales of oak and maple, sassafras and sourwood, poplar and hickory, birch and magnolia. The best of our language, I often think when I walk the mountains, is in our names for things, unadorned by any adjectival need for beauty and unused by verbs. When sunlight got overhead, a redolence was released from underfoot, a spicy odor faintly laced with something of spring and summer, liberated by my heavy steps into the chill air, where it disappeared on the breeze around me.

I far more expected to see black bear than wolves. Even before the first wolf release in October, it had been a great year for bears, or rather for seeing bears, since the animals themselves were hard-pressed by a mast failure that took hold across much of the southern Appalachians, a consequence of late frosts the previous spring. First soft mast failed to materialize in summer—blueberry, blackberry, grapes fruited poorly—and then the woody meat of hard mast hung undeveloped in the nut-bearing hardwoods—the oaks, hickories, and buckeyes did not produce. That sent *Ursus americanus*, long-suffering omnivore of the eastern woods, down from the more remote places in the mountains to the lower slopes in search of food. By late fall you could not turn a bend of trail without catching at least a glimpse of a bear, usually a female with a cub or two.

Backcountry black bear, at least where they are no longer hunted, are not especially wary. If you are walking into the wind and not making much noise, you can, intentionally or unwittingly, raise a bear's head from its business grubbing under a log or snuffling for acorns. If there are cubs about, they are softly grunted off without much ado and seem to understand which direction they are to take, usually uphill over the nearest ridge. Then the female slowly quarters uphill toward where its young had disappeared, as if she were drawing a diagonal across the slope. What I remember most clearly from such encounters is the silhouette of each retreating animal as it tops the ridge and briefly stops, as almost every one of them does, to turn that solemn Slavic face alongside its near shoulder to make sure I am not following.

Before the possibility of wolves slipped back into these woods, it was seeing bears that took you back in time. Bear enlarged the woods in a way deer did not and reminded you of the old fullness here. Black bear, like red wolves, seemed to appear and disappear through a rift in time that you might encounter along the silent trails that wound around these mountains, trails that were so fine to walk in the cold months when a constructive solitude lay on the slopes and time seemed to hang still over the brown glow of the forest floor.

But I moved no bear that morning, only solitary high-country deer whose startled attention, when they saw me watching them, reminded me of the wolves. I howled where the trail made its final bend away from Anthony Creek, thinking one of the wolves might still be up in the head of the watershed, and howled again along Bote Mountain Road for the pleasure of it, but got no response in either instance. I walked the modest summit of wolf country south for a few miles enjoying the way the big gray ridge underfoot tacked to one side or another of the trail, opening stupendous views into North Carolina and Tennessee. The stunted beech, yellow birch, and chestnut oak were spare and oriental in their beauty, each shaped like an elder gnarly with experience of many summers and winters, hard forms won from the extreme weather on the narrow summit.

I had the shelter at Russell Field to myself and that evening probably howled more than any wolf in the mountains. Wolves were well known to respond to such invitations to give voice, and I had gotten over my initial self-consciousness about doing this. Gray wolves, in fact, were more prone to answer a human voice imitating a wolf howl than a recording of an actual wolf. Their ability to make the discrimination is not as striking as their preference for real voice, even one tinged with human intentions.

People who fear wild animals or who hate them for economic reasons imagine they are everywhere. But even in wolf country wolves would prove to be scarce. The howling that morning had spoiled and misled me. As I hiked along, I assumed I was going to be listening to wolves all winter, that as long as I stayed in the backcountry I would have a sustained opportunity to learn their language. But it was, in fact, a long time before I heard them again, and, in retrospect, I was very glad I had risen, half conscious, out of my sleeping bag that morning on Anthony Creek, propped myself on an elbow, and scribbled down, as best I could, exactly what I heard.

That night there was nothing for me except a cold wind and a starry sky. I kept a small, disheveled fire of kindling and log ends going in front of the Appalachian Trail shelter until the gusting wind thrummed the ground so hard the stars shook and it got too cold to stay out. The wolf's ancient associations here with the wind and cold, with the Milky Way itself, were not lost on me. To the Yuchi, the wolf was one of the four lost sons of the wind, never where you thought it was. And silence, too, was a virtue of wolves, the most prized skill of hunting and war. The Creek answered the wolf's stealth with their own and forbade themselves even to utter the animal's name. Now that wolves were free, that dark, starlit silence within the gusts just might be the silence of wolves—not the final muteness of extinct beings, but the close counsel of animals that could be present beyond the ragged circle of the campfire, a transcendental rather than a political silence, an Emersonian silence, unvoiced echo of something that might call out.

What was left of the old mythologies was like the mountains themselves—like red wolves themselves: an old resistance that was hard to read—a mystery or a truth, a shape, a trace. I suspect I had already heard far more wolf howling than I would ever understand.

The Cherokee recognized that the excitement of the hunt might make a hunter forgetful of the prayers and formulas that justified the kill. But to neglect these rituals—the acknowledgment of guilt that propitiated the game you sought for food—was to invite trouble, excite revenge in nature, which, after all, had no use for man. So the hunter who on his way home from a successful hunt remembers that he forgot to address his game properly has one last chance to make amends. Tired and eager as he is to see his wife and home, he stops on the trail and builds a small four-log fire as a tangible sign of his debt to the life that keeps him alive and his regret at having temporarily lapsed in respect. This is called the fire in the path, an act of gratitude and propitiation. It seemed to me that mild winter night on Forge Creek, and it seems to me now, that to return red wolves to these mountains was to light a fire in the path.

Built by Fire

A couple of million years ago a pine fell in love with a place that belonged to lightning. Flying past, a pine seed saw the open, flat land and grew covetous. The land was veined with runs of water—some bold, some fine as a reed. Seeing it unoccupied, the pine imperiously took root and started to grow there, in the coastal plains of the southern United States, and every day praised its luck. The place was broadly beautiful with clean and plentiful water sources, the sun always within reach. In the afternoons and evenings, thunderstorms lumbered across the land, lashing out rods of lightning that emptied the goatskin clouds; in those times the pine lay low.

The lightning announced itself lightly to the pine one summer evening. "I reign over this land," it said. "You must leave immediately."

"There was nothing here when I came," said the pine.

"I was here," said lightning. "I am always here. I am here more than any other place in the world." The clouds nodded, knowing that lightning spoke true.

In that short time, however, the pine had begun to love the place and called out, "Please. You live in the sky. Let me have the earth." The clouds glowered and began to thicken.

Lightning was extremely possessive and would not agree to divide.

"Then do what you will," said the pine. For years they warred. The lightning would fling as many as forty million bolts a year at the tree, striking when it could, the pine dodging and ducking. A single thunderstorm might raise thousands of bolts. Wind helped the tree, and although it was struck a few times, the damage was never serious.

After the tree had reached a fair age—old enough for government work, as they say—on the hottest of summer afternoons, lightning crept close, hidden by towering maroon thunderheads, and aimed for the tree, sundering its bole crown to roots. When the lightning glanced the ground, such was its ferocity that it dug a trench wide enough to bury a horse before its force subsided. Needles from the pine had fallen about, like a woman's long brown hairs, and they began to smoke and then to flame, and from them fire spread outward, burning easy and slow.

In its dying, the pine sprang forth a mast of cones filled with seeds. The wind played with the seeds and scattered them for miles. And because the mineral soil was laid bare by fire, they could germinate.

But lightning was not worried. Kindling the whole place didn't take much effort. Once lightning struck, the fire might burn slowly through the grasses for weeks, miles at a time, arrested only by rivers, lakes, creeks, and ponds. So if the seeds began to grow, lightning would burn them.

Over the decades the fury and constancy of lightning knew no end—every few years it would burn the place again—and the greenhorn pines learned to lay low, sometimes for five or six years, drilling a taproot farther and farther into the moist earth, surviving the fast-burning, low-intensity fires of lightning's wrath by huddling, covering their terminal buds with a tuft of long needles. Sometimes the buds steamed and crackled inside their bonnets.

Young trees that mimicked grass survived fire. That low, they didn't look like trees.

The grass-trees began to learn that if they waited until the lightning went to sleep in the rainy springs and suddenly cast themselves upward, to the height of a yard or more in one season, drawing nutrient reserves from their long, patient roots, and if they hurriedly thickened the bark of their trunks, a lamination, then when the fires came again they could withstand the heat and their terminal bud would be out of flame's reach.

Only then would the trees dare to branch.

Lightning was nonplussed. No matter what it did, the trees flourished and multiplied. Admiring the courage of the longleaf pine, other trees, hardwoods—sweetgum and sumac and oak—tried to settle. Always, not knowing the secret history of longleaf's adaptation, they burned.

And then lightning realized the pine tree was plugging its needles with volatile resins and oils, rendering them highly flammable. The tree, of course, only thought to make the fires burn rapidly so danger would pass quickly. Flammability was important in driving wildfire through the forest, in order to leave older trees unharmed. The longleaf grew taller, spread farther.

The lightning saw volatility as an act of remuneration.

Longleaf and lightning began to depend on each other and other plants—the ground cover grasses and forbs, or flowering herbs—evolved to survive and welcome fire as well. Wiregrass, for instance, would not reproduce sexually in lightning's absence. The animals learned to expect fire and to adapt. They scrambled off or took cover: down into tortoise burrows, up into tree crowns. During a fire, exotic insects never otherwise seen would scurry from the plates of bark, scooting up the tree. Snakes and tortoises would dash for their holes.

Longleaf became known as the pine that fire built.

Rock Springs

As long as I can remember and until less than a year before he died, my father found his greatest pleasure in tromping through the forests he thought of as his own. His passion was the outdoors; his greatest gift to his family was sharing that love. He found it difficult to be inside, and on long summer afternoons he would pull into the driveway after work, blow the horn to announce his arrival, and command my mother, my sister, and me to join him for what he called a "daunty." Though no one else seemed to use this word—I never could find it in a dictionary—I knew exactly what it meant. A daunty is an outing in the country, one with no planned itinerary but one intended to take advantage of serendipity and to welcome the unexpected—a rattlesnake stretched out in the sun, a tree laden with ripe plums, a hedge of blackberries.

When she heard the familiar horn, Mother would quickly assemble a picnic from leftovers, and away we'd go. This often-repeated ritual continued throughout my parents' long lives, and long after we'd left home my sister and I were expected to go along for the ride whenever we visited. Some weeks after my father died and a few months before her own death, I suggested a daunty to my grieving mother, who couldn't quite bring herself to admit that Daddy was gone. As we drove down a familiar red-clay road and stopped on the banks of the Oconee River, tears rolled down her cheeks.

"Mama, you're thinking about Daddy," I observed, taking her hand.

"I've been pretending he's not dead, but it's not working anymore."

The river, the wind in the pines, the red-clay road seemed to release my mother from the denial that had gripped her since his death. The sadness of her ravaged face released a flood of memories for me.

A typical daunty on a hot summer day of my childhood began with a ride through the country with a stop by the property my father called the Burney Farm to see how the trees were growing. On the property is a natural stand of mature longleaf pines, rare survivors of the ninety million acres that once extended across the coastal plain and piedmont of the southeast. My mother, my sister, and I dutifully waited in the car while Daddy strode across the land, lingering in the longleaf, deep in thoughts that I could never penetrate. Toward the end of his life, I walked the land with him, listening as he talked about board feet, pine beetles, wiregrass, fire, and the endangered red-cockaded woodpecker.

On hot summer days the daunty often ended at a literal watering hole, a cold-as-ice spring that bubbled from deep in the ground into a basin some fifty feet across. On such an afternoon, he loved to surprise us by opening the trunk and lifting out a watermelon, which he would then with much fanfare lower into the clear, cold water of Rock Springs to cool. We always swam before eating. Diving down into the boil, we imagined seeing monsters of the deep. We dug spiral mollusks from the sand and searched the outlet stream for crawfish and min-nows. When I close my eyes, I see water oaks, yards of Spanish moss, and cypress knees pushing through the sand. After we played for an hour or so in the water, our lips were blue and our skinny bodies were chilled to the bone. We welcomed the heavy, warm air as we settled down on the sand to feast on fried chicken, cold biscuits, and water-melon. As dusk settled we returned to the water to recapture the chill that would keep us comfortable through the hot summer night.

Just as abruptly as he announced our outing, Daddy would order us into the sensible Chevrolet sedan he always drove. On such nights Mother reminded him that what she wanted more than anything was a convertible with red leather seats. Years after I first heard her half-joking request, he surprised her with just such a car—a new 1960 sil-ver Chevy Impala convertible with white top and, yes, red leather seats.

While we enjoyed the honeysuckle-scented air blowing through the car and watched the sheet lightning on the horizon, Mother and Daddy sang romantic songs, many featuring the moon:

"It's not the pale moon that excites me, that thrills and delights me. . . ."

"Moonlight becomes you, it goes with your hair. . . ."

"Carolina moon, keep shining. . . ."

"Shine on, shine on harvest moon, up in the sky. . . ."

"In the cool, cool, cool of the evening. . . ."

They seemed to know all the lyrics, and to this day, on warm moon-lit nights, I can join my voice to the memory of theirs.

After driving the thirteen miles from Rock Springs to town, we always stopped by the post office to check the mail. I wondered what my father did for so long in the P.O. He must have read his mail and left it in the box, because when he came back to the car he never brought anything addressed to him. Occasionally there was a letter for my mother, or the *Saturday Evening Post*; always there were the candy bars we had grown to expect. I don't think I ever believed that he found the candy in the P.O., but I never let on that I knew he slipped out the side door and crossed the street to a service station to chat with the attendant and make his purchases—Hershey bars for me and my sister, an Almond Joy for Mother, and Lucky Strikes for himself.

By the time we pulled into the driveway, the sky was full of stars and the heat of the day had diminished if not broken. Crawling into the twin beds in the room we shared, my sister and I must have talked, though maybe not. I remember only the night sounds—owl, cricket, tree frog, and sometimes rain. Thanks to my mother's love of storms, I was happiest when rain was accompanied by sound and light. The closer the lightning, the louder the thunder, the more I enjoyed the spectacle. To this day I feel a surge of excitement when I see lightning strike on the horizon and hear the roar of thunder.

Like many who weathered the Depression as young people, my father never had any confidence in the stock market. Whenever he had money to invest, he would buy what he called a "piece of land," fifty, seventy-five, a hundred acres of timberland in the coastal plains of southeast Georgia. Most of the land he leased to a large corporation, thinking that the annual lease money, combined with his Social Security, would provide for a comfortable old age for him and Mother. He was right, and now my sister and I enjoy that income.

When I was asked to record my father's occupation on forms for school, I never knew what to write. *Realtor* seemed my only choice, but it didn't really describe what he did. Rather than houses and office buildings, he sold farms, timberland, even swamps. My father provided for his family with money earned from the land, and he made what he called "a good living." More important to this story, however, is the profound attachment he felt for the land. A regular walk in the woods was essential to his physical and mental well-being. When he was knocked down by some ailment or injury, he would badger the doctors until they assured him that he would indeed be able to walk the woods again.

I truly believe that my father loved trees in the way that some people love birds, roses, or waterfalls. He would point out a particularly beautiful stand of longleaf pine in a reverent tone of voice, and—truth to tell—he never wanted to cut a tree. On the few pieces of land he retained for himself, he delayed harvesting the trees as long as he could, sometimes until pine beetles or drought threatened them. In the battle between monetary value of timber and the connection he felt to the forest, I can't say that either won out. He seemed to live with the tension created by conflicting values: trees for money, the woods for feeling alive. I grew up in this tension, and I live there still.

JANISSE RAY

Fire-wings

Can the fire of monarchs be blown out,
millions of orange candles extinguished
by a wild snow and a fierce wind
puffing across the Mexican sierra?

Just like that, in one cold breath,
could all the monarchs be gone?

A butterfly's body is nothing
but a notch of hollow reed
glued to scraps of paper wings.
Ardent and flammable,
it was not made to last.
One by one the monarchs stiffen and drop
from the gray masses clutched to limbs,
to the forest floor, wings shut,
until the naked firs shiver
in the unexpected winter night.

The bigger question is what
would the world be like
without their incandescence,

without the knowledge scripted
in the slender volumes of their wings?

And who would ring the bells of spring
and the bells of fall
in the bell towers along migration routes?

Who would deliver the messages of wildflowers
and converse with ditch weeds
and croon over stalks of milkweed
cradling rows of pearly eggs?

And what,
in a world without monarchs,
would set human yearning aflame?

FRANKLIN BURROUGHS

Smoke and Mirrors

Seven years ago I was invited to a gathering of southern nature writers for a long weekend on Ossabaw Island. The invitation came in the middle of a Maine winter, and I accepted with alacrity. Ossabaw turned out to be not exactly tropical—sometimes bright and chilly, and sometimes windy, overcast, and downright cold. The assembled nature writers spent a lot of time around a big fireplace in an otherwise unheated house. We had a good supply of wood, most of it live oak, deadfall from the old trees that stood around the house. Whoever got up first would gather kindling, lay the fire and light it, put on a couple of logs, and then go off to get the coffee started. By the time the coffee was done, everybody would be up, and we'd take our cups out into the room with the fireplace and find our way back into conversation.

The best of that conversation was about southern landscapes. Was there something that made them different from other landscapes? And did southern nature writing, such as it was and whatever it was, differ from other American nature writing?

We generalized and speculated. We all had strong feelings about particular landscapes and a habit of expressing them. That, and a growing sense of goodwill toward each other, was what we had in common, and it was enough. I learned a lot from what people said, and even more from what they were—where they came from and what interested them, the literal and metaphoric ground of their authority.

Every now and then, somebody would get up, go out the side door, and bring in an armload of oak and a restorative whiff of cold air. The oak was good, dry wood and burned along placidly. Occasionally the wind would gust across the chimney top, and there would be a downdraft, and the room would fill with the smell of wood smoke, which always has a kind of yearning in it.

None of us doubted that there was something distinctive about southern landscapes and the southern response to them. One of the generalizations we ventured was that southerners tend to flee from generalizations, in the direction of stories and anecdotes. Generalizations distill and depersonalize memory. Stories and anecdotes embroider it in all sorts of ways, but they do preserve it in some fashion, so that it can be served up and passed around, like pickled peaches.

And yet here we were, a bunch of southerners generalizing. We were having a conversation, and stories don't belong in conversations. A storyteller is a soloist, and a conversation is an improvisational combo.

In the years since our first meeting, books—fine books—have come from the participants in that conversation. All I have to offer from the time on Ossabaw is the usual southern thing—a memory that floated up into my mind as we talked. It was evoked by the discussion we were having, and no doubt by the fire and the smell of the smoke. This was back in the early fifties. I was about twelve years old. I grew up in Conway, at that time the heart and solar plexus of Horry County, South Carolina. Both of my parents and all four of my grandparents were born and raised in the county, if not Conway itself. This was not unusual, more the rule than the exception to it. I would stay in Conway until 1960, when I went off to college in east Tennessee. Since then my identity has been perplexed. A perplexed identity isn't bad; it simply drives home the truth of the old song: we're strangers and we're all just passing through. I have not been a card-carrying, registered southerner since 1968, when my wife and I moved to Maine, where we have at last achieved the status of resident aliens, further perplexing identity issues.

I am not homesick for South Carolina or nostalgic for my boyhood. If it had not been for reading, hunting, and fishing, I would have died there during my adolescence and gone on to a posthumous existence as a pillar of the community, a member of the Jaycees, and a middling sort of golfer. My second death, when it came, would have been respectfully reported by the *Horry Herald*; I am sure of it. My father introduced me to the hunting and the fishing. They were solemn undertakings, and had not themselves changed much over time, although many things around them had. We would be somewhere and my father would speak of something that happened there during his own boyhood, back when the roads were unpaved and people still took the steamboat down to Georgetown and the little tramline locomotives were hauling pine logs out of the swamps that were as thick at the butt as a man was tall. So in my own boyhood I was nostalgic for a county that had largely disappeared before I was born. That is one reason I am not nostalgic for my boyhood—even a southerner would stop short of feeling nostalgic about feeling nostalgic.

When I think about Horry now, it is never people or events. It is simply geography—the sandy ridges of longleaf pine, the bottomlands of tupelo and blackgum, the salt marshes and oyster banks of the swashes and inlets. The whole county was veined with branches and swamps and fingers of swamps. At the back of almost every field the land would slope down gently. The turkey oak and hickory and sweetgum of the field edge would give way to holly and loblolly pine and overcup oak as you descended, until at last you could see, through an understory of bay bushes, the gleam of dark water, the run of the branch itself. If you followed it perseveringly, it would lead you finally to a river, probably the Waccamaw, with its blackwater cypress swamps and oxbow lakes and low-water sandbars.

Southerners are always tempted to say, "Aw shucks, I ain't nothin' but a hick, if you just scrape the fancy icing off and get right down to it." But being a hick has nothing to do with geography. A hick is a species of fundamentalist, a man with one book and one book only. I sometimes envy him his unperplexed identity, but I am not that man.

I think I could say, however, that Horry County was my first book, the one that taught me how to read, to see landscape as a kind of three-dimensional narrative. Subsequent landscapes have been better reading—richer, more complex, more exciting. But I do not separate the pleasure I take in them from the memory of that first instruction.

But to get to this specific memory. I was twelve; it was a weekend in October. Daddy and I had put the boat in at Red Bluff, about twenty miles above Conway on the Waccamaw. We ran upriver another five miles or so, the little one-and-a-half-horse motor bucking the current as best it could. The river there was shallow, sandy-bottomed, and quick—redbreast water. Its swamps were wide and no farms or roads came down to it. We were going to fish that afternoon and camp out that night, and it was wild and thrilling to me.

But something was happening as we went upstream. I was a puny child and had spent a good deal of my young life lying in bed reading, with the shades half drawn and a humidifier steaming up the windowpanes like the inside of a greenhouse. The long-term effect of this would be a love-hate relationship to claustral spaces and to literature. The short-term effect was an ability to fake or disguise illness. The first phase of disguising it would be deny the first symptoms to myself. I passed out of that phase as we motored along, and knew I was getting sick. I began breathing lightly, so Daddy wouldn't hear the wheezing and cancel the trip. We got to a good sandbar and set up camp. Instead of a tent, we had two jungle hammocks—nylon hammocks with waterproof roofs and side panels of mosquito netting.

They were army surplus items designed for use in the South Pacific or perhaps an even warmer place than that. We got them strung up in some fashion, then fished until dusk, then came back, built a fire, cooked, ate, and eventually crawled into the hammocks. They were swaybacked, clammy and cold at first, and colder as the night went on. I lurched around in the hammock and back and forth across the threshold of sleep until I hardly knew or cared which side of it I was on. The wheezing gave way to coughing, as it always did.

We crawled out at daybreak, and Daddy got the fire started again. He asked me if I wanted to fish and I said no. I liked it just fine where I was, now that the night was over and the swamps were brightening. He said he would leave me with a pole and some crickets and take the boat and run upstream a way and fish back down. Then we could have breakfast and break camp and go home. Before he left, he told me to keep the fire going. There were a few logs that he had cut from a dead standing pine the afternoon before. "Save those," he said, "we can use 'em to cook breakfast."

Once he was gone, I fished for a while in the eddy below the sandbar and played at being Robinson Crusoe. By the time I remembered the fire, it was nearly out—a couple of smoldering brands in the middle of a circle of dead ashes. I went up into the woods and got an armload of pine straw, twigs, and sticks, and dumped it on the fire. That appeared to extinguish it altogether and I felt a weak, panicky despair—I had failed at the most basic skill of woodcraft, and the fire was gone and would not come back. But then a few wisps of smoke appeared, and then, with a *poof!* flame appeared. It fed greedily on that pile of skimpy fuel, and I rushed back into the woods to get more.

And so that was what my Robinson Crusoe fantasy turned into. The fire ate the fuel as fast as I could fetch it, and I had to go farther and look longer each time I went into the woods. At some point my mind began to detach itself from the practical business of what I was doing and to make a story, or a parable really, out of it. Actually it was two parables, first one and then the other.

The first parable I owed Sunday school, which was very big on parables. The fire became the uncertain, precarious shining forth of gospel truth in a dark world. Each twig, each bit of stick or straw was another convert, another brief and blazing witness to the truth. From an illustrated book in my grandmother's house, I had some hazy images of martyrs tied to the stake, wreathed in smoke and flame. That must have entered into it. My sense of guilt and despair at having let the fire go out and of undeserved deliverance when it resurrected itself also entered into it.

And then the parable shifted, in the seamless, illogical way that the scene and characters sometimes shift within a dream. It was no longer a religious parable, but for a white southern boy of my generation, it was the next thing to it. It was in front of Richmond, in the last, bitter winter of the war. There was almost nothing left—food or ammunition or blankets or troops. Everything needed to be hoarded and husbanded, but it could not be. The fighting went on every day; the lines were being pressured and extended and worn thinner and thinner. The sticks and twigs were the last scrapings of the bottom of the barrel: old men and skinny little country boys not much bigger than I was. I was one of them, feverish and chill, alone at my outpost. But I was also General Lee, wanting to conserve the little that remained and yet being obliged to feed it into a fire that ate it immediately and cried for more. The pine chunks I was saving for when Daddy returned weren't troops Lee was holding in reserve for a last desperate offensive or Richmond itself. They represented a pearl of greater price than that, an obscure sense of honor more precious than life or victory. That was the Sunday school influence kicking back in.

I don't remember how the morning actually ended. So I will say that my sleepless night and the beginnings of fever got to me, and I crawled back into the hammock, snuggled down in the sleeping bag, and at last fell asleep. And that Daddy got back, found the fire still smoldering, put the pine onto it, fanned it into a businesslike flame, and got started on breakfast. I do remember that he had half a dozen good redbreast swimming around in the fish box. And that by the time we got home again, I was ready for the bedroom, the half-drawn shades, the humidifier, and a sedating dose of literature.

Stories come from memory and become memory. They save some parts of the past, distort or delete others. A twelve-year-old African American child in 1954, any twelve-year-old child, black or white, in 2002, might make up a story while tending a fire on a Waccamaw sandbar, but I cannot make it up for them, or imagine it for myself.

The South had slavery. It also had, among the poor and poorly educated rural whites who have constituted the majority of its population for most of its history, the closest thing to a hereditary peasantry that this country has produced. Most of my family and most of the white-collar families in Conway had risen out of this class; most of the population of the county beyond the town remained in it. For me and for many white southerners of my general background and generation, the southern landscape, for all its fecundity, has a sourceless, potent sorrow in it. I cannot look at Spanish moss, swaying lightly against the softest and bluest of April skies, without feeling that something is being whispered, some admonition against too reckless and unremembering a delight in all this delectable beauty.

The nineteenth century gave to the New England tradition of nature writing a durable and adaptable philosophic premise, which was transcendentalism. It linked literary, intellectual, and political culture to the landscape. Nothing like that came from the southern nineteenth century. I think the founders of our tradition were anonymous. They were the black and white musicians, who made songs of aching defiance, despair, yearning, and homesickness that would pass into the twentieth century as gospel music, the blues, and bluegrass music.

They did not bequeath an idea upon which to rationalize a connection to the landscape so much as an emotional keynote for the experiencing of that connection.

That tradition of music has mutated, metastasized, hybridized, and gone global. It has lost about all of its geographical and historical evocation, although it still thrives in the South. The demography, and therefore the collective memory, of the whole region have changed with unprecedented rapidity over the course of my lifetime. My generation of southern white boys who grew up hunting and fishing has seen the end of something. Every generation does and it never gets any easier. But every generation also has an obligation to locate new beginnings.

At Ossabaw, we were different people, different genders, backgrounds, and generations. Southernness, even among southerners undivided by race, is a volatile basis for an allegiance. Scrape off the fancy icing, and all we were was a bunch of soloists, strangers passing through. We wouldn't have agreed about the parable of the fire, or whether it was a parable at all. But we did and do all know that what you do is you go out into the landscape. You gather up fuel. You tend a flame. And, by the logic of dreams, the flame that you tend is also the fuel that feeds it, the landscape itself.

JANISSE RAY

Butterfly

Where does its fire go
when a monarch dies?
Does it vanish
in smoke,
or turn suddenly to rain?
Does it lie dead
against a mountainside
transforming placidly
to dirt,
which will harbor in its richness
millions of small burning ships
sailing a deep-green forest,
never to be seen?
Or does the fire seep into the ground,
running in rivulets
toward the blazing core
of the earth,
one day to return:
a volcano spewing wings?

Water

JOHN LANE

First Spring Flood

What floats is all we've discarded.

ॐ

Water has a way of pure dispensation,
from each field by the laws of erosion;
to each creek according to its flow.

ॐ

Lawson's Fork curves in the willows.
Red current roils past the roots.

ॐ

Gospel truth: tomorrow frogs
will spawn in new mud.

ॐ

An old T-shirt, a baby's beach ball,
two shoes, unmatched,
a bald tire, foam in the eddies,
limbs, leaves, a dead duck.

ॐ

Lawson's Fork drops
overnight.
Water bugs gondolier
back and forth
on the clearing stream.

JANISSE RAY

For the Edge of the World

In the dead tree by the brackish pond
in pouring rain, four great egrets.

The white of them preoccupies a somber sky
with its gray sheet of rain

whistling what must be a native orchestra
among outstretched boughs of cedar,

notes ringing down stalks of spartina
and pattering into the pond.

On a clear day shrimp and minnows rise
in ephemeral circles that quickly

go silent. What can I say
I have accomplished in this life?

Can I say I stood in solidarity with the rain,
as it stormed the bilging marsh—

or that I remained loyal to egrets
on gray reaches of cedar?

Can I say my allegiance rested strong
with cordgrass?

I cannot live a quiet and simple life.
No, it must be desperate, flamboyant,

voluptuous, as if from another country,
and clumsily done. There is one small thing.

When I was in town, in the copy shop,
I met the bird artist, local politician,

whose errant gray curls plume from his head.
For a few minutes, waiting to complete

our business, we talked of birds.
The drawings he showed me were simple, and quick.

Have I stayed true to the great blue heron
balanced on one wand of leg,

evenings, in the same dead tree,
or to the wood storks

with their hindrance of bills at ebb tide?
Can I say I never abandoned them,

but was violent in my fidelity?
This: when I left, the bird-man gracefully bent,

kissed my hand, then waved me out,
into rain.

MELISSA WALKER

The White Heron

The moon was full and bright and the night was full of sound—woks, croaks, clacking, squawks, and once a piercing wail. I was having trouble sleeping, so around midnight I crawled from my tent and walked down to Eco Pond to see what was going on. *See* is not quite the right word. Even with so much moonlight, I was not able to make out the shapes of birds on the water or in the trees. No matter. Their voices told me they were there, along with frogs, insects, and other creatures singing and calling in the night. During one moment of near silence the dark shape of a medium-large bird appeared in front of me and uttered a deep-pitched squawk as it passed. The pitch of its call indicated a black-crowned night heron.

An hour later I crawled back into my tent, did battle with the few mosquitoes that had followed me in, and tried again to fall asleep. No dice. I was wide-awake and hyperalert. I looked out the mesh window of my tent at Florida Bay, where the water was still and only the slightest breeze stirred. I took up Marjory Stoneman Douglas's *River of Grass* and turned to the opening passage: "There are no other Everglades in the world. They are, they have always been, one of the unique regions of the earth, remote, never wholly known. Nothing anywhere else is like them: their vast, glittering openness, wider than the enormous visible round of the horizon, the racing free saltness and sweetness of their massive winds, under the dazzling blue heights of space. They are unique also in the simplicity, the diversity, the related harmony of the forms of life they enclose."

I read about resurrection ferns, small green tree snakes, and the now endangered snail kite that feeds almost exclusively on one species of freshwater apple snail. In the midst of a passage about strangler figs, I drifted off to sleep to wake again at 6:30 A.M. When I peeked out at the water, I spotted the great white heron with its seven-foot wingspan wheel slowly in and land on the piling usually occupied by a brown pelican. When this more homely bird arrived a few minutes later, the heron held its place while its rival circled and circled before landing in the water nearby.

The full moon was low in a pastel western sky; the eastern sky was a garish pink and orange. The tide was high and fuller than usual, but the birds arrived in their usual order, beginning with the white heron and ending with vultures. They gathered among the mangroves to wait for the water to recede and expose the mudflats where they fished.

Then came the children: two boys eight or nine years old loaded with fishing gear took over a spot near the birds and me. In a matter of minutes the smaller of the two boys had hooked what turned out to be a medium-sized eel. By the time they reeled it in, it had wrapped the line around its body several times and seemed hopelessly tangled. Sure that they had caught a snake, the frightened boys cut it loose and left it still alive and writhing in the shallow water.

I explained that what they had caught was an eel, not a snake, and that they should at least remove it from the water and bury it. Otherwise a bird, perhaps the heron or the brown pelican, would surely eat it, swallow the hook and line, and eventually die. But my chiding had no effect. The boys stuck to their story: they had caught a snake, and they weren't going anywhere near it.

I jogged to the nearby ranger station to report what had happened, but the young man I talked to was not very interested.

"We don't have the personnel to handle this kind of problem. Besides, the eel could do some damage to anyone who tried to free it."

"Well, couldn't someone at least go talk to the boys about responsible fishing? You know, explain to them that if they hook something they should remove the hook and if they can't do that, take the animal out of the water?"

"I'm sorry, but we really don't have the man power to do that sort of thing. If I talked to every fisherman who needed talking to, I wouldn't have time for anything else." With that the ranger began fingering Hemingway's *The Green Hills of Africa*, which he had been reading when I interrupted him.

I headed for my morning walk around Eco Pond and for a while forgot about the eel. About three-quarters of the way around I noticed a great white heron with a fishhook hanging from its beak. In a few minutes I was back at the ranger station reporting yet another animal in distress. The story was the same.

"There's really nothing we can do. The bird would never allow itself to be caught," the ranger explained.

"Couldn't you watch it, wait for it to get weak, and then catch it? Throw a net over it, maybe?" I asked.

"No, we really don't have anyone who can do that. Besides, it takes time. The bird would never cooperate."

"Since you said it 'takes time,' that must mean that it's possible to catch the bird and remove the hook before it dies," I persisted.

"Well, I guess it is possible. Folks down on Sanibel Island—a group called CROW—rescue a lot of birds, but we really can't do that here. You have to understand, this happens all the time."

Remembering the time that the evening news was dominated for days by the drama of two whales trapped under an ice floe, I realized that people would rally by the millions to save animals when they are large, charismatic megafauna and when the media dramatizes their plight. But if death is common, if it "happens all the time" as it does after oil spills or as a consequence of irresponsible fishing practices, we throw up our hands and say that the job is too big. If we saved one heron, we might be expected to save them all. To solve this problem, fishermen would have to change their habits, taking care to retrieve fishing lines when bait is taken by what they consider undesirable life-forms; rangers would have to enforce the rules and regulations that are so widely ignored in the Everglades. I met no one in the glades who would even talk about taking on this project.

Park rangers and administrators seemed to be stuck in resignation. "There's nothing we can do about the fishermen" had been generalized to "there's nothing we can do about anything"—about an eel, a heron, or any other wildlife damaged or killed by careless people. Later I talked to Carol Lowenstein, the staff rehabilitator at CROW, the Clinic for Rehabilitation of Wildlife on Sanibel Island. She told me that, indeed, wounded birds can be helped and that with the help of two staff veterinarians as well as student interns, they treat 3,700 birds and animals a year, about half of which are successfully restored to the wild. The difficult part of the work is capturing animals, which often can't be accomplished until they are too weak to escape—and sometimes too sick to recover.

I returned to the bay to check on the eel. It was gone, and so was the great white heron that regularly patrolled the water where the eel had been. Had the heron eaten the eel? Was the heron I saw at Eco Pond the one that sailed in to my campsite every morning? If so, then wasn't I partly responsible, since I could have found a way to remove the eel from the water and dispose of it out of reach of the birds? But like the boy who caught it, I was squeamish and thought a professional should do the job. At the information center I talked to Steve Robinson, the ranger who seemed most knowledgeable about wildlife in the Everglades. When I described the eel, he concluded that it was probably a spoon-nose eel, a common breed in Florida Bay. Steve also warned that since the eel was in distress, it might have bitten anyone who tried to rescue it.

Late that afternoon I wandered down to the marina, where two young women were trying to catch a pelican that had something large lodged in its throat. Nearby was a shed where fishermen cleaned their fish. Disregarding the small sign warning them not to feed the birds, some fishermen tossed fish remains to the pelicans that line up on pilings nearby. These birds have no trouble swallowing a good-sized live fish, which slides cleanly down their large throats. But a bony carcass often gets caught, and unless it is removed, the bird will die. It's no small job to catch a pelican and remove a fish carcass from its throat, but these young people who worked in the canoe concession regularly patrolled the area to identify and help any birds in distress. The rangers, the young woman told me, rarely take the time to help, and no one enforces the rule, Don't feed the birds.

Back at Eco Pond in the late afternoon, I waited along with a group of birders for the flocks of ibises to arrive. As I wandered along the shore, I found myself wondering which bird would be the next victim of a fishhook. Then I spotted a rarely seen sora rail creeping along the edge of the cattails. Just as the rail disappeared in the reeds, a flock of white ibises appeared overhead, and right in the middle was a flash of red as bright as the vermilion flycatchers I'd seen in the West. Just in time I raised my binoculars, and there it was. "That, madam," I heard a nearby birder say with a British accent, "is the rare and wondrous scarlet ibis." He told me that eggs from this glowing red South American bird were brought to Florida from the Caribbean in the 1960s and placed in the nests of white ibises. The experiment failed to produce a new generation of scarlets, as the transplanted hatchlings matured mostly to breed with the white ibises, producing a small population of rosy hybrids. But at least this one survived.

I woke about 5:30 the next morning. Waiting for dawn, I sipped tea and scanned the horizon. The stars were still out and the moon was low in the west, but both soon faded as the eastern horizon began to lighten. Then I saw white wings swimming through the heavy air, and in moments the great white heron landed in front of me as if it were standing for inspection. I sighed with relief when I realized that there was no fish line dangling from its beak. "Reprieve," I thought. My bird had not eaten the eel, and at least for now it was free to feed and preen in this small part of Florida it had staked out as its own.

Looking at the bird I thought of as my own, I laughed at myself as I recalled how the previous day had begun with my fruitless if not foolish attempts to save the tangled eel and the white heron with a fishhook in its throat. The impulse I'd felt to save these two doomed creatures was intense, but misdirected. Far more important, I realized, was saving the Everglades themselves so that all creatures there would have a chance to survive.

By the end of the two weeks I spent camped on the shore of Florida Bay, I had begun to think of the thousand or so square feet around my tent as my personal territory. I had readily resumed the simple life I had fallen in love with during my first three months on the road. I could look out at water, mangrove islands, sky, and birds without seeing any other humans. I was virtually alone, a condition I'd learned to cherish. To restore my spirit, such solitude seemed necessary. My days were all my own.

ANN FISHER-WIRTH

Sweetgum Country

Billy shows us his arm, burned by the sun
where pesticides sensitized his skin
those years of his childhood, playing
in Delta cotton fields. A charred,
hand-sized lozenge marks the tender crease
inside his elbow. Alex holds up her chart
that shows the sickness and death
in her mother's family, from cancer
in Cancer Alley. She has made red circles
for "fought," green crosses for "died,"
she has put stars around her name,
my pretty dark-haired student.
They come to class, my sixteen freshmen,
and no matter what their topics,
they all say, "I never knew this. . . ."

Fords and Chevies that will barely crank
one more time are parked in the reeds
and slick red mud. Early evening sun
pours down on the cypresses and sweetgum,
the Tallahatchie swamp at the edge
of Marshall County. Turtles poke their heads up.
Cottonmouths zipper through black water
or stretch out long and bask on the abandoned
railroad bridge. Men and women of all ages
beguile the hours after work,
the idle hours, with soft talk or silence,

with bamboo poles and battered coolers.
They could use the food.
They fish for buffalo, catfish, bass,
despite the fish advisories, the waters laced with mercury.

BILL BELLEVILLE

Diving into the Heart of a Poem

By late May, the warmer weather has already coaxed the man-
atees out of the thermal protection of Blue Springs and into the St.
Johns River. I have seen manatees underwater before, have had them
actually approach me as some manatees—like people—are simply
more curious. We have hung there together in the clear water, briefly
studying each other, and I have been struck with how human the ani-
mal's eyes seem, pensive and recessed inside a starburst of deeply
etched wrinkles. It's almost as if there is a person inside all that insu-
lation. Perhaps the animal thinks likewise of me—that there may be a
manatee hidden in there somewhere, under all that neoprene.

Today, the shallow run of Blue Spring here in east central Florida is
filled with snorkelers, their skin raw and goose-fleshed, splashing
among the mullet and bass, gar and tilapia. I watch this from a board-
walk at the top of a natural basin that encircles the headspring.

From up here, the cobalt water below seems to pulse, shimmering
with the electricity of the earth itself. I've been drawn to springs like
this since I was a child. For me, it's never been enough to simply watch
the world unfold. I have always yearned to be immersed in the mys-
tery of it all, to see for myself what's around that next bend, inside that
mysterious tree-line break in the canopy of the woods or that dark
cleft in the rock.

Along with a dive buddy, I gear up with air tanks, and after a stren-
uous slosh against the upstream current of the run, fin away from the
shallow sandy bottom, out to where the spring churns at the surface.
Sinking below, I navigate through a giant fork created by two fallen
logs. Under me, the cavern plunges sharply and then angles gradually
into a black chasm in the limestone. The eighteenth-century Quaker
naturalist Billy Bartram once sat on the banks of Blue and later wrote
in wonder of the "diaphanous fountain" that surged below him. Entire

tribes of fish vanished into it—where did they go, and why? There was magic here, like nothing he'd ever seen. His descriptions of springs along this river inspired the romantic poet Coleridge to write of Kubla Khan, where Alph the sacred river ran, through caverns measureless to man, down to a sunless sea. I would give all I have if Bartram could be next to me today, could feel the full sway of this natural "ebullition," down here inside of his spring.

As I go, I must fin hard to push against the fierce upwelling of Bartram's ether, cool current pressing my mask deep into the flesh of my face. Looking closely in the soft rock around me, I see subliminal clues to the prehistoric sea that accrued to form first the platform, and then the crust of Florida. The clues are fossilized shells, still ribbed like a scallop, or cupped round like a clam. They are welded together by the dust of Eocene coral, whale skull, oceanic sand, an assemblage of calcium turned white as bone. I am traveling into the cellar of Florida, descending past ledges protruding from the rock, walls sculpted like gentle, vertical waves by a prehistoric water flow. I bump into one ledge, and as I push off, I feel the softness of it, more marly clay than hard rock. At sixty feet, where the muted surface light fully disappears, a metal sign warns divers without special training to go no farther. It reads simply: Prevent Your Death.

I've been schooled in the peculiar behaviors of cave diving, so I turn on my underwater light and let its beam pull me downward. It seems puny, dim, nearly absorbed by the darkness. Scuba tanks, face masks, containers of light—they're all reminders of how unsuited we humans are to travel inside the most primal element of all.

The water I swim against is cool enough to chill me inside my thin wetsuit. I take my regulator out and gulp a mouthful. It is pure, with the vague taste of a sunless sea.

Like other springs, Blue is recharged by rainfall seeping down through rocky fissures and fractures upland from here. As the weight of the water in the rock builds from above, the water below seeks out faults and fissures where it might escape. Indeed, if the caves are the capillaries and veins of our aquifer, then springs and sinks are the natural incisions through which it most clearly expresses itself.

But the journey of water through the rock is not a straight or easy one, and the delay between the time rain falls from the sky and emerges from the limestone is wondrous. Elsewhere along this river, hydrologists have dated the age of spring water. At Croaker Hole, a dark, river-bottom vent I will later visit, water has been trapped in the rock for 3,900 years. At Salt Springs, for 7,000 years. Perhaps the water I taste now once fell as rain when the earliest Native Americans who lived here were still alive, even fell on and around them.

The pre-Columbian Timucua had a word for this water. *Ibi*, they called it, and it was cool and eternal and everlasting. They drank it, bathed in it, paddled their dugouts across it. Their reverence for *ibi* was not separate and apart from their life, but woven into it—as sure as the rise of the sun and moon over the wild Florida landscape.

It disturbs me that we moderns, with our science and our human conceits, are convinced we can solve all our problems with just a little bit more technology. But the truth is we are taking out more water from this aquifer than nature is putting back in. Florida is big, driven by growth now, and our thirst is great. For the first time in our history, the liquid energy that once shaped the destiny of this entire peninsula is now being shaped by us. We have taken ownership of *ibi* away from the gods, and in doing so, affected the enchantment of the watershed itself.

And, if water has lost its sacredness, can mere human law ever atone for it? I often wonder if there is penance for violating such inviolability, wonder if we can ever be fully redeemed for mistakes of this scale. I have no easy answers—after all, I am not a politician—so I do what I can. And now, all I can do is to breathe, in and out, and down here in the darkness, let the rainfall of the Timucua consume me. I turn myself over to it, wanting to give it all that is in my power, but knowing, ultimately, I can promise only reverence.

At 120 feet, the force of the water surging out of the limestone crevice below is massive. Even if the throat of the cave were larger, the power of its flow would keep me from going farther inside. At this depth, the pressure of the water above gives me the vague feeling of being shrink-wrapped.

I hold on with both hands to a boulder near the darkest hole and let the energy coming from it blow my body up and away, suspending my torso in the swirling ether, flailing my legs.

I'm deep inside Bartram's diaphanous magic now, my exhaust bubbles rising like domes of mercury and becoming part of the upwelling roil of Alph that swells and—finally—drifts away to the surface. Off it flows, this confluence of spring water and poetry and exhalation, past the tribes of humans and fish, down the spring run, to the river, and toward the sea.

CHRISTOPHER CAMUTO

Water

Downstream of Chilhowee Dam, the Little Tennessee bends around the foot of Chilhowee Mountain opposite the mouth of Citico Creek. Freed from the task of incising the hard rock at the heart of the Unakas, work that kept the river busy throughout the Cenozoic, the Little Tennessee casts itself in broad loops through what was once the valley of the Overhill towns. Before the gates of Tellico Dam were closed and that final stretch of the river lost beneath another feature-less mask of still water, students of the river read its twists and turns as well as its abandoned meanders and terraces, inferring from what they found the signature of shifting Quaternary climates.

The living river built nine alluvial surfaces here, in addition to its modern floodplain, a process driven by the rhythm of glacial advance and retreat hundreds of miles to the north. Although glaciers never reached the southern Appalachians, each stadial pushed a finger of cold south along the mountains, creating a peninsula of northern plant and animal species. During the coldest centuries, the lower slopes of the Unakas were covered with jack pine and spruce. An alpine zone of tundra and permafrost took hold above 4,500 feet. The highest peaks were bare, windswept regolith.

During full glacials, the frost action generated by periglacial cold ground the exposed bedrock of the Unakas into unstable debris that eventually sorted itself out into colluvial fans unfolded onto the mountainsides above the river. The interglacials brought rains that washed that rock downslope until it became grist for the river's mill. Eventually the heavy load of gravel, sand, and silt settled out in the river's bed or was deposited on its banks. When sediment loads decreased, the river would abandon its floodplain, which eventually left a landscape of nested alluvial terraces. At some point in the late

Quaternary, the river stopped its broad meandering and settled into a more stable, braided flow around persistent islands.

Human beings drifted into the valley twelve thousand years ago, about the time the climate eased during the start of the current interglacial. During the early Holocene, another load of frost-churned rock washed off the slopes and the river built the most recent terrace. The boreal climate retreated, withdrawing the life it favored. Tundra and caribou disappeared, as did spruce grouse and most of the spruce. The mountains reforested themselves in response to a warmer, wetter climate with the stunning variety of deciduous trees that survived the Wisconsin glaciation in lowland refugia. Beech, poplar, oaks, hickories, maples, walnut, ironwood, basswood, and elm were waiting in the wings. This new vegetation stabilized the slopes and built soil. The amount of sediment reaching the river decreased once again, and the last terrace was complete. The Little Tennessee abandoned that last terrace for its modern floodplain between three and four thousand years ago, about the time the Cherokee language was separating from its Iroquoian parent stock.

The floodplain and lower terraces of the Little Tennessee River preserved a luminous sequence of objects abandoned to time, artifacts that stretch the imagination: from palm-size Clovis and Dalton points of Paleo-Indians, who scalloped their edges with antler tines and thrust them at the trailing edge of Pleistocene megafauna, to the symbolically incised gorgets of the Mississippian people, who taught themselves the dimensions of the quadripartite universe.

Plant-fiber baskets left their weave on the fired clay hearths of the early Archaic, which also stranded notched spear points and chert butchering tools—knives, hammerstones, scrapers, drills, gravers, and cobble net weights—as well as nuts and seeds gathered from forests and savannas. The middle Archaic made better points, short-stemmed and more easily hafted, refined the lithic tool kit with which meat was butchered, and fashioned cylindrical and crescent-shape stone weights for the throwing stick the atlatl—which levered a spear with dramatically improved velocity. Cobble weights were notched to anchor fishing nets more securely. Large, broad-stemmed Savannah River points appeared along with grooved axes and celts of the late

Archaic. Fragments of steatite bowls confirm the permanent settlement indicated by charred rinds of squash and gourd, the first of a slowly developing sequence of cultigens that shaped civilization here.

Ceramics anchored Woodland period settlements, vessels refined over time by improved tempering mediums—crushed quartzite, sand, limestone. Spear points became arrowheads—small, efficient chert triangles. Stone tools were ground and polished to a beautiful sheen. Mortars and pestles marked an increased use of mast, seeds, and wild plants—maygrass, knotweed, lambsquarters. Trade goods turn up—exotic Adena and Hopewellian ceramics and prismatic blades of Ohio chalcedony acquired for cut sheets of mica and soapstone quarried from the surrounding mountains. Wild marsh elder was cultivated and then maize appeared, the tiny cobs a strange gift from the sun. Wood-structure settlements broadened. Forests were cleared.

Crushed mussel shells tempered Mississippian ceramics. The deadly arrowheads de Soto's men felt were fashioned, along with steatite ear spools, negative-painted effigy vessels, stone and copper plaques. The startling images of the Southern Ceremonial Cult that adorn these things seem to come out of nowhere—bird men and serpents, big thunder and falcons—but a fabulous subconscious had been here all along. Important imaginations lived along this river, imaginations that lent transcendental significance to these material objects. Ceremonial mounds squared the center of large palisaded villages graced with plazas and wood-frame council houses and dwellings of wattle and daub. Within the palisades was kinship and ceremony; beyond, the world of hunting, trade, and war.

Then the Overhill towns of the Cherokee occupied these ancient sites. According to *Adair's History of the American Indians*, published in 1775:

> Their towns are always close to some river, or creek; as there the land is commonly very level and fertile, on account of the frequent washings off the mountains, and the moisture it receives from the waters, that run through their fields. And such a situation enables them to perform the ablutions, connected with their religious worship. . . . They are . . . strongly attached to rivers,—all retaining the opinion of the ancients, that rivers are

necessary to constitute a paradise. Nor is it only ornamental, but likewise beneficial to them, on account of purifying themselves, and also for the services of common life,—such as fishing, fowling, and killing of deer, which come in the warm season, to eat the saltish moss and grass, which grow on the rocks, and under the surface of the waters. Their rivers are generally very shallow, and pleasant to the eye; for the land being high, the waters have a quick descent; they seldom overflow their banks, except when a heavy rain falls on a deep snow.

November now, at Citico, the color failing in the hills. I say Citico, but facing the gray, pockmarked chop of Tellico Lake, I'm not so sure. It's cold and raining lightly. I'm chilled and feeling the weather and tired of searching out things I can't see.

Featureless as the lake is, for a Cherokee, the land here is still well marked. Downstream you can see the great cliff where the *tla'nuwa'*, the great hawks, once nested. "They were immense birds, larger than any that live now, and very strong and savage." In the old time, they wreaked havoc on the people until a medicine man of Citico defeated them, much like Odysseus, by playing one form of negation off against another. He fed their nestlings to the *Ukte'na*, a monstrous serpent that dwelt in the water below the cliff. The enraged hawks pulled the *Ukte'na* from the water and tore it to pieces in the air. The scaly chunks of the snake fell to earth and scarred Chilhowee Mountain, and the hawks departed. Upstream was the favorite haunt of *Utlun'ta*, Spearfinger, a woman clad in stone who fed on human livers.

Despite the myths that add an imaginative dimension to this landscape, I can't get beyond the prosaic. I'm at a well-trashed boat landing where a sign riddled with bird shot warns me not to drink the toxic water or eat any fish from the shapeless lake that now covers the ruined valley of the Overhills.

There was a current from the release at Chilhowee Dam, a mile upstream, but the wind canceled that out, so I paddled easily across the main channel a hundred yards to an island shaped like a fishhook opposite the landing. Huge suckers or carp darted away on my approach, leaving puffs of disturbed silt in the calm shallows along shore. I looked for peach orchards and river cane but saw mostly alder, birch, and willow, the latter holding slender yellow leaves over the water like lures.

Another sign warned me not to steal anything, that this ruined place was now protected. There might be artifacts that escaped the mechanical sluice boxes of the salvage archaeology done here in the shadow of the construction of the Tellico Dam, and there still may be soulless people who come to steal what's left of the past here, but the officious, red-lettered sign seems a bit hypocritical, since the culture that posted the warning also built the dam. As it was, if I had come to steal from Citico, there would have been no one to stop me. But the thieving here—five hundred years of it—is pretty much done.

When I turn the upstream end of the island, I'm pleased to see two bald eagles perched in the upper branches of one of the drowned snags where Citico was. The golden eagle was the revered bird of the Cherokee, the war eagle whose feathers were sacred objects, but the unmistakable head and tail of its cousin is a heartening sight on eastern rivers, as affirmative as seeing bear or wolves. As long as the great birds don't eat any fish from Tellico Lake, they will be fine.

I paddled closer to the eagles, slowly and obliquely so as not to spook them. A corridor of snags and stumps off to my left marked the old channel of Citico Creek, which had made this an especially desirable place for twelve thousand years. I got within fifty yards of the birds and, when they flew off downriver, rousting crows from the shore, I circled their perch, hoping to find a feather. But the taking of eagle feathers is not a casual affair, and there was nothing on the water.

From the base of that tree, I saw the world from what was left of Citico—the broad expanse of water covering what had been the confluence of Citico Creek and the Little Tennessee, the steep rise of Chilhowee Mountain, a large island downstream that would have been part of the town. Underneath me was a world—burials and postholes of homes, middens and gardens, a mound and a council house with a fire burning at the center of a red-clay hearth. A wolf's tooth with a hole drilled in it, as if it had been a pendant, had been found among the ruins.

Lieutenant Henry Timberlake came to Citico in December 1761, having descended the Holston River from Virginia and then poled his way up the Little Tennessee with bloody, blistered hands, trying not to fall too far behind his Cherokee escort and lose face with the vanquished. The English had tried to use the Cherokee as pawns in their war against the French, but the strategy fell apart in what became an international blood feud. The war between the Cherokee and the English had ended with a treaty signed in November 1761 on the Long Island of the Holston by Timberlake's superior, Colonel Stephens. Timberlake carried the articles of peace to the all-important Overhills, who had requested that an English officer appear in person among them to settle the matter.

After taking in the ruins of Fort Loudoun, the first English fortification among the Overhills, which the Cherokee had captured in August 1761, Timberlake presented the articles to the war chief Ostenaco at Tomotley and then to the assembled chiefs and warriors at the council house of Chota, center of the nation and keeper of its principal fire. The peace was smoked and then followed by ceremonial dances and a feast of venison, bear, and buffalo.

Timberlake then received an invitation to come to Citico (called Settico in Timberlake's journal), at the time the most belligerent of the Overhill towns and deeply implicated in the hostilities. They flew two white flags for the Englishman from the top of the council house but received him as a people justified and, in some respects, vindicated by the recent war. Timberlake describes his reception:

> About 100 yards from the town-house we were received by a body of between three and four hundred Indians, ten or twelve of which were entirely naked, except a piece of cloth about their middle, and painted all over in a hideous manner, six of them with eagle tails in their hands, which they shook and flourished as they advanced, danced in a very uncommon figure, singing in concert with some drums of their own make, and those of the late unfortunate Capt. Damere.

The unfortunate Damere, along with twenty-five others, had been brutally executed after the successful siege of Fort Loudoun, blood vengeance for the murder of an equal number of Cherokee hostages by the British and one of the last great assertions of the law of clan revenge. This meeting with the English officer at Citico was, therefore, a great moment for the Cherokee, who were still, like the French and English, a nation. The details of it were well etched on Timberlake's mind.

The headman of Citico met Timberlake in front of the town house, "holding an old rusty broad-sword in his right hand, and an eagle's tail in his left." His body was painted red, except his face, which was half black, the visage of war and death, one of the great masks of Cherokee life.

They danced the eagle dance here at Citico for Timberlake and danced it as if they thought all Europe were watching. The violent gestures, pounding dithyrambs, and raucous shouts of the Overhills ended with their chief swinging that rusty sword just over Timberlake's head and striking it with all his might into the ground within inches of the Englishman's left foot. While the hilt quivered, he made a short, emphatic speech to the stunned young man—which Timberlake's interpreter told him, tongue-in-cheek I assume, was a hearty welcome. The chief then gave him a string of beads, which was either a peace offering or an insulting talisman for all the cheap trade goods that had undermined the traditional Cherokee way of life and put them on the path to dispossession.

Then it was over.

Timberlake was led as an honored guest into the darkness of the council house, where he was blinded until a circular fire of river cane flared up and revealed the faces of five hundred warriors staring at him from an amphitheater of benches. The chief of Citico addressed him again, this time in a tone of friendship, and Timberlake was given another string of beads, this one a true gift, a token of the open-mindedness of these people. Then the eagle dancers entered and finished the dance, which symbolized a manly progression toward peace and reason.

I much wanted to see these things, but they were gone. Citico was gone. And even the place where Citico was—the bank of a river near the confluence of a bold stream—was gone. Strange, this process of erasure, this removal that will not stop.

I turned my back on the empty expanse and paddled through the rain toward the mouth of Citico Creek, losing my way in thickets of cattails that closed in warrior ranks along the shore—Cherokee, Mississippian, Woodland, Archaic, Paleo. A cattail perhaps for every man or woman who had speared a fish or snared a duck here, or who pretended to go for water to meet a lover after dark. Twelve thousand years of North American history so easily named. You would think that every speck of that deep, intriguing past would have been pre-served, including the shape of this place, that the creek and the river would have been left intact, the old languages honored, and the sur-rounding forests and mountains treated with respect, if not reverence. Strange. Maybe it was the rain, but the arrogance and waste in the air was awful. The marsh grasses rattled and I was cold.

I found the creek mouth. The creek was full and still. The sky bright-ened, the rain eased. It seemed warmer. I heard geese far off on the lake behind me, gabbling as if in response to the changing weather. The creek and the fine-grained rain made the world seem small, as if there were nothing beyond what I could see. There was no wind, just the quiet surge and drift of the canoe, the hull ticking distinctly against each leaf in its path, the trees beyond the cattails nearly bare, a little bit of everything left—a few leaves, a few birds, the tail end of the year drifting off. I seemed to have found the proper scale of things.

Citico Creek looped gracefully inland, narrow and deep, dark green. Eventually I saw current stream faintly around a sunken branch and a near-perfect thing came alive, flowing. The paddle came to life against the quickening current, the shaft straining at the throat with each deep pull. I flushed two ducks just past the upper end of a small island, slate-blue birds with white showing in the trailing edge of their wings. As I watched the empty air, trying to remember them, a dozen more burst from the opposite bank in a sustained commotion that also ended before I could gather the entire fact of it in my mind.

I paddled as infrequently and slowly as I could through the V of sky in the water that separated the image of the closing banks, savoring every nook and moment. The mallards I had flushed reappeared in flight, gaining altitude in a loosely organized chevron of their own. Then a pair of wood ducks broke from behind an overhang of willows. Then the creek made a sharp turn to the left, narrowed, and the cur-rent stiffened until I could make no headway against it. I let the current turn me just below a deadfall of sycamore and drifted back out on the deep, dark water of Citico Creek.

I've not been in a finer place. The richness of life Timberlake described seemed still to fill this quiet corridor. The universe seemed balanced there between water and sky, motion and stillness, expectation and surprise. Time and space eddied in the soft currents of Citico Creek, autumn shorn into fall. Migrant songbirds, oblivious to the rain, hung onto drooping seed heads of marsh grass; pileated woodpeckers cried from out of sight, as if to clear the woods of anything that wasn't going to winter there. The moving water created a direction between the still banks of the known world. Every dead leaf seemed to be going somewhere.

That night I made camp in the rain on the south bank of the great Cherokee River between Citico and Chota. I slept under my canoe like a warrior and dreamed dreams. In the morning I paddled through a mist that danced in sheets on the river like the borealis. Above Bacon's Bend, a raft of what must have been a hundred or more Canada geese suddenly appeared around me, silent as if I were still dreaming. Odd the way they floated there and started their preflight gabbling only after I had paddled through them and then, though I knew it was about to happen, froze my heart with a thunderous communal takeoff that left the river in terrific silence.

I beached the canoe and fell asleep again on the grassy bank until the sun woke me. At Chota you are out of sight of the mountains and surrounded by an open, low-slung horizon befitting a peace town. Chota, too, is gone now, except for a spit of land bulldozed out into the water where there is a halfhearted memorial to the Overhill towns that had been destroyed so many times. A circle of concrete pillars marks the place, one for each Cherokee clan, the remembrance already pitted with weather and acid rain. The pillars are cut obliquely so that the top is an oval on which a clan name is inscribed in English along with a simple image—Deer, Wild Potato, Wolf, Paint, Bird, Long Hair, and Blue. Which is to say *Ani'-Kawi', Ani'-Gatage'wi, Ani-Wa'ya, Ani'Wa'di, Ani'-Tsi'skwa, Ani'-Gila'hi, Ani'Saha'ni*. The semicircle of clans is turned south, as is the river for a short stretch, toward peace and Wahala, the White Mountain. In the middle of the clan totems there is an oblong trough, full of rainwater and small stones when I saw it.

The spit of land reaches to the grave of Oconostota, "Great Warrior of the Cherokee," whose bold life from 1710 to 1783 spanned the last victories and the great loss of land. It is supposed to be a great tribute that he was not inundated along with his people. His bones and burial goods were raised and reburied here to spare his grave from the polluted waters of Tellico Lake. He was buried in his canoe, along with his knife, iron cup, siltstone pipe, and eyeglasses. He was given a western gravestone on which is inscribed a prayer stick image of a warrior. Beyond this grave the river bends west again, out of sight, toward *Usunhi'yi*, the Darkening Land, and the ghost country, *Tsusgina'i*, where the spirits of the dead dwell. There were cattails on Oconostota's grave, disheveled by the wind, but I think they had been laid there. I added yarrow, for peace, and a branch of blood-red sourwood.

Downstream of Chota there is nothing really. Ghosts and the ghosts of ghosts. A slight memorial to Chota's sister town Tanase, acknowledging the appropriation of its name for a river and a state out of another comic slippage of syllables—Tanase, Tanasee, Tunisee, Tunissee, Tannassy—none of which the Cherokee ever applied to the river, the indigenous name for which remains uncertain. And then the spiritless suburban world opposite Toqua and Tomotley, a hum of lawnmowers and traffic up and down Tellico River and Ballplay Creek.

And Fort Loudoun, painstakingly reconstructed, and moved to high ground. Some things, apparently, are worth preserving. The fort appears as if the Cherokee had never conquered it—palisade and bastion, face and flank, parade ground and hornwork, glacis and moat. Great care was taken with the reconstruction—the spiked logs of the palisade tilted out at the prescribed fifteen-degree angle and the moat thickly planted with black locust, stiff-limbed and thorny.

The evening I passed by them the water between Fort Loudoun and the Tellico Blockhouse, across the way, was moved only by the evening breeze. There was no Cherokee River. The hearths and graves of Tuskegee lay under water a few hundred yards offshore, invisible. Upstream and down, there was nothing. The Overhill towns were gone: Tallassee. Chilhowee. Citico. Chota. Tanase. Toqua. Tomotley. Tuskegee. Mialoquo.

Sometime just before the removal, a Cherokee patiently tried to explain the sacredness of the placement of these towns and this land-scape to a Christian missionary: "The west half of the council house was holier than the other part,—the space about the white seats was still more sacred, but the seventh post and space about it, holiest of all. Mountains were more sacred than low ground. . . . The ground on the banks of rivers and on the sea shore was more holy than that back from the water. But the ground under the water was still more sacred than that on the shore."

Now it was all underwater, but nothing was sacred here.

JANISSE RAY

The Seat of Courage

with thanks to Barry Lopez

Intrepid in her ways, the loon alone
comes to Vinal Lake, where she floats
in the torn-silk mist of summer mornings,
placid through rising mist like white fire,
these burning waters that hold the new green
of hemlock in their light.
Everywhere the blue of lupine rages.

All afternoon, into the long spill of high Yaak twilight
until there is hardly a seam to the day
the loon serenely floats.
She dives again and again
into water we can't dip our hands into
without shivering, plying the clouded bottom.

In darkness she seeks sustenance.
Trusting the lake to keep her wild
and hidden among the thick-treed hills.
Sometimes all day it rains, or days.
Night comes.

Once I came upon a softshell turtle newly killed
and, despising needless death, took it home
to eat. All night it sat in the refrigerator.
Next morning, dressing it, I found the heart
still pumping, pumping hard, though
every other part of the turtle lay stiff.
Eerily it throbbed in my hand, majestic, crazed.

The turtle did not die of failure of the heart,
mad desire of one fluttering ember within us all.

Hours afterward in a saucer of water it beat.

Let it not be said that in passing through
this world you turned your face
and left its wounds unattended.
Say, instead, when your friends cut open
your chest, to eat of its courage,
a loon was calling.

Epilogue
Why We Write

What the Creek Teaches

Until recently, much too little had been made in southern writing of what David Abrams has called "the more than human world." Most southern literature we think of as "place based" celebrates a narrow realm of landscape, the human foreground: agriculture, town and city and more recently suburban life, family, hunting, fishing, adventuring. Less has been made in southern writing of wild landscapes that stand as source for all things human.

I'm always looking for the natural form of a place: What does the land want to be given deep time? Which stretches of a landscape want to say white oak, which others say longleaf pine? Where are the low places where water gathers? Where are the high ridges where water drains away? I believe given enough time—hundreds and thousands of years—any place can recover its organic form. The vegetation reaches climax again. The soil builds. The creeks run clear.

It is in my region's water that I see most clearly my own love of wildness reflected. When I look to the piedmont's creeks and rivers I see enduring beauty over time. I see shoals and slow backwater. I see the lovely floodplains full of sycamore and river birch. It's here we can see some of the largest trees left in a region that, from the interstates and highways, looks as if it's been given over fully to development.

What's happened in the southern piedmont shows me that a place, even a place with a "sense of place," is always in danger of being surveyed, bought, and developed. It's my belief that the whole of the world cannot, should not, be bought and sold. I've never believed in the primary concepts of the "free market" extending over all; I can't accept that everything has a price, including the air, land, and water.

I often look to my own backyard—to Lawson's Fork, the creek that flows out beyond my study—to find my wildness. It is bigger than I am. It's my own little Yosemite and I walk it every day looking to be surprised and delighted.

The Spartanburg suburbs pushed in around the creek's edges in the 1960s, and it still runs red from construction runoff upstream with every rain event. It's still threatened by non–point source pollution—runoff from roads and lawns and discharge from septic fields. But I like to think Lawson's Fork is still wild at its cool, flowing core. That wildness is somewhere deep in the steady current, the migration patterns of wildlife drawn to it, the slow meander over time across the floodplain.

How do we get at that wildness? We look for it, and when we find it, as Rick Bass says, we don't let go. Writing poems is my way of hanging on. It's my practice and I'll keep at it the way the creek keeps cutting at the sandy bank on the far bend.

THOMAS RAIN CROWE

God Willing
and the Creeks Don't Rise

When I returned from the west coast to the mountains of
western North Carolina in 1979, I expected to find the relatively clean
air, clean water, and undeveloped landscape that existed here in my
youth. Instead, I found myself in the midst of the beginnings of an all-
out war on the ecology of the region, which today has escalated and
manifested itself in any number of ways and around any number of
environmentally sensitive issues ranging from EPA Superfund sites to
severe air-quality problems.

After reading and hearing about issues such as development, zon-
ing and land-use legislation, toxic waste, logging, water quality, and air
pollution almost constantly in the news, and after many years of fight-
ing the good fight with body and soul as a frontline member of a num-
ber of cultural and environmental organizations and movements, and
seeing not nearly enough positive change in this Katuah bioregion, I
took a spring trip to Ossabaw Island in 1999 at the invitation of Janisse
Ray and John Lane. I wanted to link up with the southern nature writ-
ers group that had been meeting annually for a few years to try and
address the ecological and environmental issues in the Southeast, as
well as to invigorate one another with their writing. With conditions
in the South getting worse by the year, and with politicians failing to
do anything about it, it seemed logical to me that the nature writers
needed to step up and take a position of leadership where the welfare
of the region's landscape was concerned. To wage a war with words
with regularity and with as much skillful conviction as possible.

Fueled by my association with the southern nature writers tribe, I
have pushed my poetry into prose and led my own private campaign
here in the western North Carolina mountains these past few years,
primarily in the pages of an enlightened news weekly: the *Smoky*

Mountain News. My goal: to try and elucidate the issues and bring about public debate, hoping that this will result in the end of unchecked and so-called "growth" and "development" in an area that is changing rapidly (hopefully not inextricably) and which was once a true treasure trove of biodiversity and beauty. Through a series of weekly columns and regular features, as well as in a memoir chronicling four years lived with and in the natural world and wilderness areas of Polk County during the early 1980s, I have resolved to add my voice to those of the other "new naturalists" here in the South in trying to make a difference—figuring, as has been the case over the past 150 years in this country, that it is up to the naturalists and nature writers to lead the way toward a more progressive thinking where questions of balance and sustainability are concerned.

In the words of an old Cherokee ceremonial chant: "May it continue"—God willing and the creeks don't rise—this nature-activist tradition, this beautiful place, and these people who live here well.

ANN FISHER-WIRTH

Where Love May Find Its Ground

One of the great tragedies of the present political situation—just one—is that, in the midst of the ongoing human drama, it has become increasingly difficult to focus on America's continuing environmental devastation. Our roads are widening, our trees are falling, our rivers and oceans are being poisoned. Several years ago, *Greenpeace Magazine* described the lower Mississippi river near my home as "a chemical soup beyond scientific understanding." Throughout the world, fertile ecosystems are paved over and perishing. The Bush administration seems to be doing everything it can to make sure these things continue happening. Yet many Americans want to learn about the rapidly diminishing natural world, about the possibilities for meaningful action, and about ways of life that provide alternatives to the dominant, environmentally lethal practices. As the political situation deteriorates, as our country moves through war but not toward a genuine peace, and the domestic economy continues declining, it becomes more important than ever to keep firmly in mind that there is an environmental crisis of global proportions and extreme urgency.

And it becomes more important than ever to learn about and rejoice in the place where we are—the earth, air, fire, and water of our home—what this present anthology calls the "elemental South." "The body makes love possible," Galway Kinnell has written. And poetry, which speaks to us through the vast rich kingdom of the senses, evokes for us our bodies and the body of the world. This is where love may find its ground even in a season of desolation. This is one thing that may teach us yet to desire, to know, the green world. To recognize that healing the world will require healing ourselves, our separation from the natural.

For poetry can awaken in us an awareness of value defined as something other than commodity. Ezra Pound wrote, in *The Pisan Cantos*:

Pull down thy vanity, it is not man
Made courage, or made order, or made grace,
   Pull down thy vanity, I say pull down.
Learn of the green world what can be thy place
In scaled invention or true artistry,
Pull down thy vanity.

Now more than ever we must find constructive ways to learn this.

Reasons

I write about nature because I love the land I live on. I am one of the many forms of life it has produced, another of its newborns, born pink and naked, nursing from my mother, surviving to adulthood, surviving this far. I write because I enjoy being alive on this beautiful earth, and because I love the gifts I have been given as a human, that may or may not be limited to the human species: the ability to use language, to know beauty, to communicate with other humans, to understand (with or without fear) our coming deaths, to anticipate death, to know there is a past, a present, and a future, and to be able to use information from history to reason about the future, to affect our own future.

I also write out of love for land I don't live on.

"The human race was born out of nature and it is out of nature that the human race and all of life is sustained every second of every minute of every hour," wrote Wes Jackson in *Altars of Unhewn Stone*. I write because I understand this to be true.

I write out of fascination with human powers, not simply the primary senses, but the sixth sense of intuition as well, and, I believe, dozens of other senses we have neglected: sense of direction, sense of longing, sense of pitch, sense of obligation, sense of place, sense of hostility, sense of time. And on. These are our evolutionary birthright, one I believe we are losing as we strive diligently to sanitize and pesticide and safeguard our lives, so that we are never hungry or scared or drowning or eaten alive or even bitten or stung or sick. In doing so we become weaker creatures. I am not interested in lost powers, but in living a life that hones all human powers, even those we have almost lost completely.

The world rages with wounds. The way we treat women. The way we treat children. The way some people are thought inferior because of skin color, race, nationality. The brutality of governments. Torture.

War. The way men are made to fight wars they did not start and to die in the name of patria. The way the lives of black people, native people, immigrants, and many other classes of people are diminished still. The way the noble ideals of free speech, true democracy, and justice for all have been eroded by corporate interests.

Of all the wrongs and wounds, there is none greater, in my lifetime, than the great wound we are making against nature, so that we have bored a hole in the ozone, accelerated global warming, cut most of the earth's old-growth forests, exterminated great herds of bison and flocks of passenger pigeons, sped the rate of extinctions to unpardonable levels, overpopulated the globe, caused diseases among wildlife, made native ecosystems rare by destroying them. I think there is no greater task before us, now in the twenty-first century, than figuring out how we can live sustainable, honorable, simple lives on the earth's landscapes. This is why I write, about nature, about my beloved southlands. Because I am dedicated to helping find one solution to this bitter challenge. My answer, if none other.

I write because I am angry at what has been lost, and bitterly disappointed to have not seen the ivory-billed woodpecker or heard it hammering in the tupelo bottoms.

I write because I love humanity. I love our faces and the things we say and think and do. I am sorry to see the worst parts of human beings surface and sad to see us suffer for what we have (collectively) done. Suffer we do, and will continue to do, with the loss of human life due to toxic air, water, and land. With the loss of our senses. With the loss of our knowledge of the world. I write to possibly alleviate a minor portion of the suffering.

I write because it seems fitting that one of the creatures able to use language, to pass messages across geographies and generations, should speak for those who cannot. Because life is unendingly fascinating. Unbearably beautiful. Utterly fragile.

MELISSA WALKER

Wildness in the Garden
and the Wilderness

Blossoms of kwanzan cherry and heart-shaped petals of dog-
wood cover the earth where I sit in my garden that sweeps up a steep
hill to the second highest spot in DeKalb County, Georgia. Only Stone
Mountain is higher. The hill is crowned with old-growth red oak, tulip
poplar, hickory, sweetgum, and one towering shortleaf pine. Redbud,
dogwood, sweet shrub, and witch hazel dominate the understory,
while Virginia creeper, galax, wild ginger, trillium, and Solomon's seal
are scattered about the forest floor. I like to think the top of the hill is
my own personal micro-wilderness, a place where for three decades I
have watched natural processes at work.

Here I have watched pileated woodpeckers feeding on the dead limbs
of a mature white oak, a Swainson's hawk diving to the earth and slowly
squeezing the life from a small rodent, a domestic cat leaping into the
air instantaneously killing a newly fledged Carolina wren, that same cat
and her feline companion recklessly playing with a copperhead snake, a
raccoon cautiously moving her six offspring from one tree hollow to
another, and hundreds of small mammals—rabbits, possums, squirrels,
bats—playing out their genetically programmed lives.

Through the years I have been surprised by unexpected visitors—
three rose-crowned kinglets in the garden, a summer tanager at the
bird feeder, a rufous hummingbird in the perennial bed. One winter
night, my children woke me to see a silent and ghostly snowy owl
perched on a limb just outside a bedroom window.

On spring nights I hear the barking, cackling, gurgling ruckus of
barred owls and the muffled hooting of great horned owls. Deepest
summer brings the deafening chorus of katydids. The sounds of crack-
ling thunder are especially intense at the top of this hill, and one sum-
mer afternoon I watched a bolt of lightning strike and split the trunk

of an ancient tulip poplar, jumping from there to a nearby loblolly pine. Recently a strong winter wind brought down a great white oak bringing along with it a good-sized red maple. Accustomed to violent night sounds, I slept through it all.

On this hill, about five crow-fly miles from the state capital, I have been able to witness day by day the cycles of botanical nature as seeds sprout, grow, flower, fruit, decline, and die. Almost every day that I am at home I spend some time in my garden, where I watch the cycles of life and death play out before me. But I periodically leave my garden to spend time in wild places. From the Everglades to the interior of Alaska, I have spent hundreds of days hiking down trails where large predators roam and I am potential prey, and as many nights sleeping on the ground trusting that my own death might be but is probably not imminent. The common thread for me in these very different experiences in nature is a perpetual consciousness of mortality, a state of mind that mysteriously feeds my own life force and brings me now predictable moments of joy.

As I sit on a spot of earth covered with pink and white petals and surrounded by royal and Christmas ferns pushing up fiddleheads, wild azaleas in full bloom, mountain laurel showing color, memories of springs past come and go. Surrounded by this prodigal floral display, I close my eyes and relive the events of an April morning in 1980 when the inevitability of death in life was written indelibly on my soul. My husband went out for his usual morning run, and when he failed to return, I began to worry. After alternating between anger and anxiety, I felt a surge of relief when he finally came through the door and into the garden. Then I saw his pale face and a shirt covered with what I soon learned was someone else's blood. In the almost quarter century since that day, the scene he described returns to me every April. Here are the words I wrote that morning:

I wish I had been the one to wake at dawn
To run through a haze of pollen-filled air
through deserted streets
painted pink and white with blossom.
Then I would have been the one to stop in my tracks

at the scene of an accident, the smell of blood
and the sound of rasping breath.
Chilled with the truth of draining life,
I would have known firsthand
the heartless deception of a pristine dawn
indifferent to an unconscious boy
painting the pastel flower-strewn canvas with his own blood.

I go to my garden as to the wilderness, looking for joy and solace that comes from the undeniable confirmation of mortality, and in my bones I sense how birth and death and everything in between are contained in a fading flower and a broken, bleeding body. With each new encounter with wild nature, I come closer to letting go of self to merge with all there is.

FRANKLIN BURROUGHS

The Place of Writing in the World

I think that if the whole kit and caboodle of us—Janisse, Jan, Bill, Chris, Susan, Ann, Thomas, Melissa, John, Rick, Jim, and I— could agree on anything about being southern nature writers, perhaps this would be it: it's strictly amateur—a vocation, maybe, but not a profession. There is no money in it, no training for it, no academic infrastructure, and no strong regional tradition of it. The writing, however much informed by reading, education, and specific research, grew out of parts of us that were more or less accidental and truant. It grew out of childhood knocking around, out of curiosities that nobody particularly encouraged, out of vacant lots and hedgerows, a bit of swampland or marsh that snaked its way up into backyards, or a creek that ran, lucent and sweet, down behind the automobile dealership at the edge of town.

Think of those sorts of places. They are overlooked. Nature, abhorring a vacuum, steps in. The first thing you know, critters start showing up there—salamanders, a snapping turtle, a muskrat, a barred owl, and (yes, Virginia, there are such things and they thrill our little souls with fear and wonder) a strange pattern of delicate tans and beiges in the sun-dappled shade of a ditch bank that magically resolves itself into a small copperhead, its tongue slithering in and out at you, politely inquiring about your intentions.

Small serpents included, these are places of a certain kind of genesis. You follow the ditch bank, the marsh, the stream, the string of woods, and it leads you on, and that is all you ask it to do.

Nature writing is a bit like that. It isn't poetry or fiction or journalism; it isn't philosophy or religion. It grows up in ground they don't cultivate, expands where they contract, contracts where they expand. From their perspective, it looks unprepossessing, yet its subject is finally bigger than theirs, surrounds them the way the countryside surrounds the suburbs and the city. The creek behind the automobile dealership is part of a drainage that shaped historical patterns of settlement. That also carries another kind of history—wastes and toxins and politics and other evidences of original sin—downstream, away from the backyards and into the future. That finally reaches the sea. It leads you on.

CHRISTOPHER CAMUTO

Becoming Southern

The path that took a writer from Brooklyn, New York, to Sewanee, Tennessee—where I am writing these words on the porch of Rebel's Rest at the University of the South—can't have been a straight one. But it's good to know that life can still shape itself, if you let it, like a meandering river or a mule path, a slow, stubborn, casually relentless progress toward where and what you want to be.

I fell in love with the South through its language. I remember reading Thomas Wolfe's long, slow, casually relentless sentences during study hall in a suburban Long Island Catholic high school in the late 1960s. *Look Homeward, Angel* it must have been. The suburbs, safe and comfortable, didn't look like much to me. I needed nature. I think I also liked the way the seriousness of religion, not my cup of tea even then, was carried by passionate—some intellectuals would say too passionate—prose that read like it had grown out of a sweet, sad landscape I hadn't even seen yet. The meandering mulishness in Wolfe's rivers and the gentle rise and fall of his blue mountains seemed as noble a backdrop for the human comedy as any in literature. Wolfe, of course, led to Faulkner, and then I was sunk. I liked the South's sentences from the start.

In a fit of rebellion against my education, I worked construction after college and then took my blue-collar grubstake to live on Chincoteague Island and later Webb's Island farther down the Eastern Shore. Those were happy days, beginning to become a Virginian. I did some serious, responsible work on behalf of the Shore's migrant farmworkers, but my secret trade back then was writing very bad fiction, stories as callow as my young self. But while I was being a fool, the land worked its way with me and a few honest sentences of my own were beginning to form in the back of my mind. By the time I got to western Virginia, I was ready to try my own language on the earth, air, land, and water that had captured my attention in high school.

In another fit of rebellion—this time from the gnawing abstractness of graduate education—I accidentally wrote a nonfiction trilogy on the southern Appalachians, three books in which I grew and then molted versions of myself as a would-be southerner lost in the land. Add the volume of verse on my desk and my environmental writing and there are a thousand published pages—good, bad, or indifferent— on the southern mountains that caught my young eye and mind and heart before I had ever seen them.

You can't love southern nature in a literary way without fighting for it against the forces that destroy it. Those forces are legion and grow- ing. So the South has also made me ardently political and led me to battles over the abuse of public forests, the needless damning of rivers, the ongoing pollution of our air and water, and a long list of other familiar, unsolved issues. Now, no longer callow I hope, I'm turning back to verse and fiction, not because verse and fiction solve problems, but because they might shed light on the deepest causes of those prob- lems—the tragic necessity of our self-destructiveness—and show me other aspects of myself I wandered south to find.

Claim Staked

For me writing has always been a journey and an exploration. Twenty years ago, when I first started writing essays about the natural world, my greatest thirst was to learn about nature's character, especially the fragile filigree of relationships that connect the earth's species. Every fact I gathered from scientists confirmed what I'd come to suspect in my outdoor ramblings: that the beauty and health of our world hang on a complex set of relationships humans barely understand. My job, I thought, was to bring this fact to light through accounts of my explorations.

Nature still fascinates me. And there continues to be a vital need for a literature of pure natural history. But more and more I have found myself pulled toward telling stories about people in their landscapes, especially their sense of place and how it affects who they are. Even in cities our natural surroundings have profound effects on our state of mind. The smell of a spring rain, the movement of clouds, the fall of light in late afternoon—all these things help shape our psyches and determine whether or not we feel at home in the world.

I grew up in suburban Delaware, among deciduous forests that were being systematically cut for development. When I was twenty-three I moved to western Oregon, where I fell in love with the fir-lined mountains and rocky coast. But something curious happened there. Although I had a good job, made close friends, and met the man I was to marry, although I dearly loved to explore the countryside, I never managed to relax in Oregon. Something about the place felt wrong to me; I was constantly ill at ease. After a few years we moved back East, settling in Atlanta until an opportunity for me to write a book took us to Hatteras Island on the North Carolina Outer Banks.

We intended to stay on Hatteras only a year or two, long enough for me to finish the book. Once again, though, the landscape had other plans for me. As I explored the wide beaches and buggy marshes, as I worked alongside fishermen and scientists, I came out of myself. It seemed as if I had spent my previous years sleepwalking through life. We've been here eighteen years now and have no plans to go anywhere else. At night I lie in bed and listen to the maritime wind whooshing through the loblolly pines that surround the house, and feel a peace that eluded me in my early life. Logically my attachment to this landscape makes no sense, but it's an undeniable fact. What's more, the coast is not the only southern landscape to hold a strange power over me. In Oregon's fresh volcanic peaks I felt lonely and displaced. But whenever I manage to spend time in the battered old Appalachians, I return home feeling washed clean by leaf-filtered light and pouring streams.

Why have the southern mountains and coast claimed me? What other intangible relationships do people have with the natural world that go unheralded in this culture? Finding stories about this region that I love, drawing them out, and putting them on paper is a way to honor them: all of this has become a main quest in my writing journey.

SUSAN CERULEAN

Writing the Birds

According to ancient myth, cranes showed humans the alphabet by imprinting the marks of their toes in soft clay. With the land's body as tablet, those long-legged birds taught us how to write.

I began my tutelage under the native birds as a young field technician working on the coastal plain of South Carolina. I sat with my boyfriend on his rough screened porch, focusing cheap binoculars on a feeder just outside. Number one: a small noisy creature with an ebony cap and throat. A chickadee, of course; hadn't I known this bird all my life? But my new bird list asked, "Is it the black-capped or Carolina version?" I had to learn the difference, and as I did, I recorded it on the checklist with an *X*, just as the crane had instructed.

An unusually cold winter delivered brilliant cardinals, startling evening grosbeaks, and blazing yellow goldfinches to the sunflower seeds we provided. Check. Check. Check. The simple marks meant I was there. I had seen these miracles and responded. We would circle the total number of a day's sightings at the top of the list, counting and recounting. Thirty kinds of birds, then forty. I wanted to find more. Flipping through Peterson's *A Field Guide to the Birds*, I noticed its organization by families containing similar, related species. If I could locate all the ducks commonly occurring in South Carolina, I could add twenty or more checks to my list.

A coworker left a guide to the waterbirds of North America on my desk with a small note affixed: "Learn!" And so I made my way through the ducks that first winter, squinting to distinguish their profiles in flight against the lowering sky of the coastal marshes, and memorizing the distinctive plumages of male and female where they differed. Common loon. Red-breasted and hooded merganser. Blue-winged teal. My favorite: the shoveler. Observing these things closely is how I learned to love, as well as to write.

On weekends, with my friends, I stalked berry-laden clumps of wax myrtle, checking off yellow-rumped warblers and ruby-crowned kinglets. Over the fields we learned to pick out the tilt of the wintering marsh hawks, and on the telephone wires, the kestrels. Each a part of my adopted landscape. Each as if it had never before existed. Or maybe it was my eyes that had just suddenly focused. Where had I been looking all my life?

My experiences of birds as a child were surprised sorts of encounters, chancy moments, unpatterned. In kindergarten, I was taught songs about orioles and robins singing sweetly in the spring, but no one knew or could convey the seriousness, the dependability, the pattern in their return. My family lived season to season, loving the natural world, but not fully aware that we were actually of it. Now, on my first Christmas Bird Count, I tallied flocks of robins in the bitter cold swamps. According to the park's bird list, robins only occurred here from November through March. All my growing years in the north, I had seen robins, but thought them only simple worm-pullers in suburban yards, never before in context: as members of the thrush family, seasonal travelers through time and space, deserving of the highest order of awe.

With my coworkers at the biological field station, I crossed and recrossed the rivers of the coastal plain, listing and checking off not only the birds, but trees, rare flowers, bog-dwelling pitcher plants, and orchids. Once named, the fallow fields leaped into sharp relief, no longer anonymous blurs of color but stands of tiny cornflower-blue toadflax, and the coarse, rosy heads of sheep sorrel, mixing like a palette by Monet. I came to count on their annual emergence in the resting fields along our route to the coast, with brilliant phlox and verbena at their feet. In the same way, we learned to anticipate the black-throated blue warbler and the common redstart, and put ourselves in the path of their northbound migrations in April or early May, noting from the range map that they travel back every year from the tropics to breed further north.

I was possessed with the abundance of what I saw, the numbers, and the numbers of kinds. It was a crash course in the most essential kind of sight, the beginning of looking for things within their proper context, coming to see how life weaves into a particular landscape. Our lists began to coalesce as we groped into an understanding that birds occupied particular places or habitats, at most particular times. On Bulls Island in May, we found the nonpareil—a painted bunting—singing high in the canopy of an old live oak. Neither the check box nor the margins of the bird list could contain all that I felt and wanted to say about that bird's embodied glory. I bought a gray clothbound field notebook and began to keep detailed notes on what I saw, and where and when. My *X*s and checkmarks lost their primacy, slowly evolving into story.

Since that time, writing has become an ever-larger gesture for me, the act of laying my language against life and attempting to match it, beauty for beauty. Writing is how I contain and pass on the privilege of living on a nonrandom planet. Writing is my bow to the crane.

RICK BASS

Losses and Gains

As an expatriate in the mountains, I am connected now to the South mostly by memory, and by the travels of birds—the blazes and arrows of migrating warblers and vireos, returning each year, and leaving again—and by my own travels, returning a few times each year to the place where I was born and raised. And I am connected also by the past, and to the green and yellow southern landscape that first taught me how to be a writer.

I live now in a landscape of wild physical and sociological amplitudes, but one of the things for which I am most grateful to the South is the incredible support that landscape provided me when I was first beginning to write. The organic philosophy of the South influenced me—swamp rot, jungle heat, and fecund floral excess. I know I was shaped by the drama of bounty and the biological understanding—or naive belief—that in such a landscape, even when things go bad, they can recover. That the South is a land, almost always, of dynamic growth and productivity; which is its own form of forceful amplitude. Slash a scar into the skin of the West and it might remain there for hundreds of years. Make a mistake in the South, and you might still know absolution within your lifetime. The botanical and organic vigor of the South creates a condition that is conducive to nurturing and supporting the extravagant world of possibility in which many writers thrive.

The downside to such a milieu, of course, is that a culture of non-reverence can proliferate. If a tree can grow big again in forty or fifty years, why get all hot and bothered about sawing them down? What currency does mystery and rarity have when the green roar of the jungle is so quick to race in over, and obscure, poor choices?

Westerners, I suspect, are more inclined to look at the natural world as a line in the sand, with every day a fierce and holy battle—we still have the opportunity to perform triage, we still possess a handful of big wild places that can still be saved intact—while the skills of a southerner might often be better utilized summoning the old ghosts and dreaming of a reconstructed future in which ecological passions are fierce and wild rather than muted and downtrodden. In the West, we still have—barely—our grizzlies and wolves, caribou and wolverines to rally our spirits toward wildness. In the South, in many places, such rallying and template making will be up to the spirits of humans, almost exclusively. What a burden that is, and what a responsibility; and what an amazing opportunity. Southerners get to start over because they *have* to.

The South's recovery will have to be done grove by grove, and story by story, poem by poem, and easement by easement. But it can be done.

If I lived in Florida, or say, Alabama or Tennessee—or indeed, perhaps anywhere in the South, these days—I believe I would already be crazy, so dramatic is the loss of speciation and unique habitat in those places. It is going to take every ounce of imagination that can be mustered to dream up happy futures for these beleaguered island-places. For a person who loves the creation—the mad joy, the extravagant, divine logic of butterflies and salamanders of all different colors, hues, and vibrancies without quite understanding their meaning—the future is a terrifying place, even in the exuberant, forgiving South.

As the West is wide, the South is deep, rich with layers of human time and history. One of the great things about the South is that if your own near past does not interest you, you can carve deeper, dive deeper, into any of the fecund histories, real or imagined, on which you stand: even as the ecological history on which these cultural and personal histories are founded erodes. All literature is about loss, and hence, indeed, the South stands waist-deep in literature.

Clearly, then, the contrarian thing to do, the rebellious thing, is to imagine, and then attempt to execute, a literature of gain, and of reclamation. It would not be the first time that vast and ongoing loss has kindled such a desire; but clearly, it is time again. Where is the restraint in this disposable society of consumption and ravenousness? Where are the small and tender gestures that once comprised the fabric of a life? Perhaps this literature of gain or reclamation can be accompanied by subtle but powerful and steady reformation, or perhaps it will move more quickly—more revolutionary—in nature.

When I write about the South, I am tempted toward, and succumb often to, the lure of my own sweet past, thirty and forty-five years distant, perhaps because the present is too terrifying to look at with full and complete clarity.

But even in the presence of such queasiness, I like to believe that if I were still living in the South, I would be able to look past the moment and participate with the new generation of writers to build structures as well as dreams—dreams and plans of reserving and creating open spaces—which is to say possibilities—into the future. To encourage new *possibilities*, rather than foreclosing on old dried-out and gone-away ones. This is not the duty of art, but there's no rule that says we can't do it this way—as I think the contributors in this collection recognize—and for that, I'm grateful. Their task is huge, and their charge—like the land itself—sacred.

BILL BELLEVILLE

The Un-Manifesto

Take a Hike

Can we as writers truly see nature by glorying ourselves as the note takers and perception makers of a story? It is presumptuous to do so, yet it happens all the time. Sitting here to write about wild places—instead of exploring them—is a construct, a dalliance, a trick. It is a way of fooling readers into thinking there is something more important to do than to become immersed in the natural places that once were our homes.

Get serious: no one is going to save a place because we tell them to do so. That's disingenuous, like telling a young child he should breathe in and out in order to stay alive. Humans know, deep in our souls, we ought to preserve the natural world because we came out of it. But our clever human intellects and our egos put up complex defenses. We fool ourselves into rationalizing. We think there's plenty to go around, because there always was.

People will save nature because they connect with it in some way. Maybe we can help them connect—but only if we don't become so enamored with our own voice. Yammering on just makes people who already think like us feel avenged. The average reader—who likely won't be reading essays like this anyway—is going to need more than words to change his or her mind. If our mission is to be in service to humanity—and to the landscape in which it lives—we need to sneak up more carefully on the cognitive process. A light tap on the shoulder works well. So does a whisper in the ear. A shout in the face may make us feel good, but it has the opposite effect on the reader who endured the shouting.

For me, then, the intent is to try to get deeply inside of a place, to become intimate, full face pressed right up against it. Perhaps I do this because I am driven by some guileless kidlike need to know. But I don't have to break my quest down to the last molecule—and then adore myself for having done it. I just need to examine, to act, and then to tell the story of it. Afterwards, I move on to the next adventure, just around the bend. If I've done my job, maybe readers will be outdoors immersed in their own intimate discovery by then.

Aldo Leopold said it: we can be ethical only in relation to something we can see, feel, understand, love, or otherwise have faith in. More recently, Jim Harrison said the danger of civilization is that we piss away our lives on nonsense. Self-absorption is nonsense, a behavior born from glorifying the same ego that separates us from nature. Put down this book right now. Go outside, maybe inside a stand of cypress or to the edge of a blackwater river, and breathe deeply. Let the sweet mystery of the natural world do its work. You don't need us.

Author Biographies

RICK BASS is the author of more than a dozen books of fiction and nonfiction, including *The Sky, the Stars, the Wilderness*; *The Book of Yaak*; *The Lost Grizzlies*; and *Fiber*. The stories in Bass's first short story collection, *The Watch*, won the 1988 PEN/Nelson Algren Award in 1988, and his novel *Where the Sea Used to Be* won the James Jones Fellowship Award.

BILL BELLEVILLE is an award-winning environmental writer and filmmaker who lives in Sanford, Florida. He has traveled widely on assignment for research including the White Sea of Russia, the Great Barrier Reef, the Amazon Basin, and Central America. His book *River of Lakes: A Journey on Florida's St. John's River* has been described as "a natural and cultural history reminiscent of Thoreau's *Walden* or William Warner's *Beautiful Swimmers*." Belleville's most recent book, *Deep Cuba*, chronicles a marine biology expedition to that country's coastal waters.

FRANKLIN BURROUGHS grew up in South Carolina and now lives in Maine, where he teaches at Bowdoin College. His book *The River Home: A Return to the Carolina Low Country*, chronicles a canoe voyage through the Carolinas on the Waccamaw River. His account of this distinctive and rapidly disintegrating backwater reflects on life on and off the river, topography, and how this landscape echoes in the speech, memories, and circumstances of the people he encounters.

CHRISTOPHER CAMUTO is the author of *A Fly Fisherman's Blue Ridge*, *Another Country: Journeying toward the Cherokee Mountains*, and *Hunting from Home*. In addition to new nonfiction, he has a volume of short stories, a novel, and several volumes of verse in progress. He teaches in the English Department at Bucknell University.

SUSAN CERULEAN has written and advocated for wildlife conservation from her home in Tallahassee, Florida, since 1981. She edited *The Book of the Everglades*, *The Wild Heart of Florida* (with Jeff Ripple), and coauthored *The Florida Wildlife Viewing Guide* (with Ann Morrow). Her essays have appeared in several collections and many publications, including *Orion Afield* and the *Miami Herald*. In 1997, she was named Environmental Educator of the Year by the Governor's Council for a Sustainable Florida.

THOMAS RAIN CROWE is a poet, translator, editor, publisher, recording artist, and the author of ten books. Among his recent books are *In Wineseller's Street: Renderings of Hafiz* and *Water from the Moon*. Crowe lives in Cullowhee, North Carolina.

JAN DEBLIEU makes her home on Roanoke Island, on the Outer Banks off the North Carolina coast. She is the author of *Wind: How the Flow of Air Has Shaped Life, Myth, and the Land*, winner of the John Burroughs Medal for nature writing. Her previous book, *Hatteras Journal*, is a vividly rendered account of the rigors and rewards of dwelling in a habitat where only the most resilient forms of life manage to prevail. She also is the author of *Meant to be Wild*, a nonfiction book about captive breeding programs. DeBlieu currently serves as the Cape Hatteras Coastkeeper.

ANN FISHER-WIRTH is the author of *William Carlos Williams and Autobiography: The Woods of His Own Nature*, published in 1989. She has published many articles on American writers, among them Willa Cather, Robert Hass, and Cormac McCarthy. Her poems have appeared in the *Georgia Review*, the *Kenyon Review*, *Feminist Studies*, *ISLE*, the *Southwest Review*, the *Valparaiso Review*, *Flyway*, and the *Florida Review*. Her first book of poems, *Blue Window*, was published by Archer Books in September 2003. In 1988 Fisher-Wirth began teaching at the University of Mississippi in Oxford, where she is currently professor of English.

The late JAMES KILGO was the author of *Deep Enough for Ivorybills,* *Inheritance of Horses* (both essay collections), and the novel *Daughter of My People.* Kilgo's essays appeared in the *Gettysburg Review* and other literary magazines as well as in the Sierra Club anthology *American Nature Writing 1996.* His last book was *Colors of Africa,* which appeared shortly after his death in 2002.

JOHN LANE has been published in *American Whitewater, Southern Review, Terra Nova,* and *Fourth Genre.* In addition, he has been anthologized in *The Heart of a Nation* and *A Year in Place.* His books include *Waist Deep in Black Water,* among several volumes of poetry, and *Weed Time,* a gathering of essays. He was coeditor of *The Woods Stretched for Miles: New Nature Writing from the South.* Lane is an associate professor of English at Wofford College, in Spartanburg, South Carolina.

JANISSE RAY is the author of *Ecology of a Cracker Childhood,* winner of the Southeastern Booksellers Award for Nonfiction in 1999, the Southern Book Critics Circle Award for nonfiction, and the Southern Environmental Law Center Award in 2000. A naturalist and environmental activist, she has published essays and poetry in *Wild Earth, Orion, Florida Naturalist,* and *Georgia Wildlife* and is a nature commentator for Georgia Public Radio. Her most recent book is *Wild Card Quilt: Taking a Chance on Home.*

MELISSA WALKER is the author of *Living on Wilderness Time,* in which she chronicles two hundred days spent alone in America's wild places, along with two other books, *Reading the Environment* and *Down from the Mountaintop.* She serves as vice president of National Wilderness Watch, chair of the Georgia chapter of Wilderness Watch, and serves on the Southern Appalachian Council of the Wilderness Society. She has been a professor of English at the University of New Orleans and Mercer University and a fellow of Women's Studies at Emory University.

CPSIA information can be obtained at www.ICGtesting.com
Printed in the USA
LVOW12s0431220813

349023LV00001B/19/P